CHINESE LOVE SIGNS AND RELATIONSHIPS

TUNG JEN

quantum

LONDON • NEW YORK • TORONTO • SYDNEY

quantum

An imprint of W. Foulsham & Co. Ltd
The Publishing House, Bennetts Close,
Cippenham, Berkshire, SL1 5AP, England

ISBN 0-572-02517-3

Printed in Great Britain by
St Edmundsbury Press Ltd
Bury St Edmunds, Suffolk.

CONTENTS

Chinese Animal Year List

OPERATIVE DATES	ELEMENT	SIGN
February 18, 1912, to February 5, 1913:	Water	Rat
February 6, 1913, to January 25, 1914:	Water	Ox
January 26, 1914, to February 13, 1915:	Wood	Tiger
February 14, 1915, to February 2, 1916:	Wood	Rabbit
February 3, 1916, to January 22, 1917:	Fire	Dragon
January 23, 1917, to February 10, 1918:	Fire	Snake
February 11, 1918, to January 31, 1919:	Earth	Horse
February 1, 1919, to February 18, 1920:	Earth	Goat
February 19, 1920, to February 7, 1921:	Metal	Monkey
February 8, 1921, to January 27, 1922:	Metal	Rooster
January 28, 1922, to February 15, 1923:	Water	Dog
February 16, 1923, to February 4, 1924:	Water	Pig
February 5, 1924, to January 23, 1925:	Wood	Rat
January 24, 1925, to February 11, 1926:	Wood	Ox
February 12, 1926, to February 1, 1927:	Fire	Tiger
February 2, 1927, to January 21, 1928:	Fire	Rabbit
January 22, 1928, to February 8, 1929:	Earth	Dragon
February 9, 1929, to January 28, 1930:	Earth	Snake
January 29, 1930, to February 16, 1931:	Metal	Horse
February 17, 1931, to February 5, 1932:	Metal	Goat
February 6, 1932, to January 24, 1933:	Water	Monkey
January 25, 1933, to February 13, 1934:	Water	Rooster
February 14, 1934, to February 2, 1935:	Wood	Dog
February 3, 1935, to January 23, 1936:	Wood	Pig
January 24, 1936, to February 10, 1937:	Fire	Rat
February 11, 1937, to January 30, 1938:	Fire	Ox
January 31, 1938, to February 18, 1939:	Earth	Tiger
February 19, 1939, to February 7, 1940:	Earth	Rabbit
February 8, 1940, to January 26, 1941:	Metal	Dragon
January 27, 1941, to February 14, 1942:	Metal	Snake
February 15, 1942, to February 3, 1943:	Water	Horse
February 4, 1943, to January 24, 1944:	Water	Goat
January 25, 1944, to February 11, 1945:	Wood	Monkey
February 12, 1945, to February 1, 1946:	Wood	Rooster
February 2, 1946, to January 21, 1947:	Fire	Dog
January 22, 1947, to February 9, 1948:	Fire	Pig
February 10, 1948, to January 28, 1949:	Earth	Rat
January 29, 1949, to February 15, 1950:	Earth	Ox
February 16, 1950, to February 5, 1951:	Metal	Tiger
February 6, 1951, to January 25, 1952:	Metal	Rabbit
January 26, 1952, to February 13, 1953:	Water	Dragon
February 14, 1953, to February 2, 1954:	Water	Snake
February 3, 1954, to January 23, 1955:	Wood	Horse
January 24, 1955, to February 10, 1956:	Wood	Goat
February 11, 1956, to January 29, 1957:	Fire	Monkey

Chinese Animal Year List

OPERATIVE DATES	ELEMENT	SIGN
January 30, 1957, to February 17, 1958:	Fire	Rooster
February 18, 1958, to February 6, 1959:	Earth	Dog
February 7, 1959, to January 27, 1960:	Earth	Pig
January 28, 1960, to February 14, 1961:	Metal	Rat
February 15, 1961, to February 4, 1962:	Metal	Ox
February 5, 1962, to January 24, 1963:	Water	Tiger
January 25, 1963, to February 12, 1964:	Water	Rabbit
February 13, 1964, to January 31, 1965:	Wood	Dragon
February 1, 1965, to January 20, 1966:	Wood	Snake
January 21, 1966, to February 8, 1967:	Fire	Horse
February 9, 1967, to January 28, 1968:	Fire	Goat
January 29, 1968, to February 15, 1969:	Earth	Monkey
February 16, 1969, to February 5, 1970:	Earth	Rooster
February 6, 1970, to January 25, 1971:	Metal	Dog
January 26, 1971, to February 14, 1972:	Metal	Pig
February 15, 1972, to February 2, 1973:	Water	Rat
February 3, 1973, to January 23, 1974:	Water	Ox
January 24, 1974, to February 10, 1975:	Wood	Tiger
February 11, 1975, to January 30, 1976:	Wood	Rabbit
January 31, 1976, to February 17, 1977:	Fire	Dragon
February 18, 1977, to February 6, 1978:	Fire	Snake
February 7, 1978, to January 27, 1979:	Earth	Horse
January 28, 1979, to February 15, 1980:	Earth	Goat
February 16, 1980, to February 4, 1981:	Metal	Monkey
February 5, 1981, to January 24, 1982:	Metal	Rooster
January 25, 1982, to February 12, 1983:	Water	Dog
February 13, 1983, to February 1. 1984:	Water	Pig
February 2, 1984, to February 19, 1985:	Wood	Rat
February 20, 1985, to February 8, 1986:	Wood	Ox
February 9, 1986, to January 28, 1987:	Fire	Tiger
January 29, 1987, to February 16, 1988:	Fire	Rabbit
February 17, 1988, to February 5, 1989:	Earth	Dragon
February 6, 1989, to January 25, 1990:	Earth	Snake
January 26, 1990, to February 13, 1991:	Metal	Horse
February 14, 1991, to February 2, 1992:	Metal	Goat
February 3, 1992, to January 21, 1993:	Water	Monkey
January 22, 1993, to February 9, 1994:	Water	Rooster
February 10, 1994, to January 30, 1995:	Wood	Dog
January 31, 1995, to February 18, 1996:	Wood	Pig
February 19, 1996, to February 6, 1997:	Fire	Rat
February 7, 1997, to January 27, 1998:	Fire	Ox
January 28, 1998, to February 15, 1999:	Earth	Tiger
January 16, 1999, to February 4, 2000:	Earth	Rabbit
February 5, 2000, to January 23, 2001:	Metal	Dragon
January 24, 2001, to February 11, 2002:	Metal	Snake

CHINESE ASTROLOGY AND LOVE

The origins of Chinese astrology are lost in the mists of time. It is known that, in the West, some sort of study of the stars and planets was being undertaken several thousand years before the Christian era and Chinese astrology is at least as old.

All branches of astrology relate to the workings of our own solar system and all are based on a series of 'patterns' which the ancient people considered they could make out amongst the backdrop of stars. In the West, these groups of stars, spread out roughly around the equator of the Earth were named after Gods, Goddesses and heroes of epic tales. The groups of stars are known collectively as the Zodiac.

In the wide skies of China the original watchers of the heavens chose more or less the same patterns of stars for their own Zodiac, but for reasons that we do not quite understand, they chose to give them animal names. The number of possible interactions between the Sun, Moon and planets, even across a short period of time is quite staggering, so having the reference point that the Zodiac offers was clearly a distinct advantage. It was discovered that the position of the Sun, Moon and planets within the Zodiac at the time of any person's birth had a bearing on the nature and life of the individual concerned.

CHINESE CYCLES

In China a particular number of planetary cycles, amongst a host of possible ones, came to be seen as the most important. Most significant amongst these was a 12 year cycle and a 60 year cycle. Since there were 12 animal signs in the Zodiac, each successive year was named after one of them. Each year was also said to be ruled by an 'Element' and there were 5 of these, so the whole process could only come full circle after 60 earth years had passed.

The ancient Chinese set great store by each animal year, believing that the type of animal ruling the year in question would have a bearing on human affairs generally. The Element responsible for the year in question also had a bearing, they believed, on people's lives and political events.

THE MOON AND ASCENDANT

Eventually it was realised that a person born under a particular animal and Element combination would carry certain traits. These were studied and catalogued across hundreds and possibly thousands of years and formed the basis of Chinese personal astrology. However, the Chinese were also very tied to study of the Moon, which they used as a basis for constructing personal horoscopes. Along with this they noted the 'Ascendant', or 'Rising sign' which is that part of the Zodiac that is passing across the Eastern Horizon at any particular point in time.

THE SUM TOTAL

Taken altogether the basic components: Animal Year, Element, Moon Sign and Ascendant, formed a potent and accurate picture of the nature of any person born on the Earth. No marriage would be arranged, business agreement made or house built until the astrological happenings of the moment had been calculated, for astrology ruled events just as surely as it did people.

Only fairly recently has all of this become generally known in the West and many comparisons have been made in the last decade between Chinese and Western branches of astrology. The basic difference seems to lie, in the main, in the care that the Chinese took to allocate the correct animal type for each sign of the zodiac. So well do they fit differing types of people that one is left astounded, not only by the Chinese ability to understand astronomy and astrology, but also by the clear insights these peoples had concerning the natural world around them.

Since every sphere of life is subjected to the caprices of the the Sun, Moon and planets, a very accurate system of computation and interpretation developed, and this has come down to us in its present form as a result of thousands of years of patient observation. Any person choosing to study the results in detail can be left in no doubt that the ancient Chinese were amongst the most skilled astrologers of any period or culture. They treated interpretations with obvious humour and were greatly interested in knowing what made a given person 'tick'. Even to the modern eye there is a great connection between the animal signs of the Zodiac and the resultant natures of those ruled by them.

THE SPHERE OF LOVE

In *Chinese Astrology* all areas of life were examined; in this book, as the title suggests, we focus mainly on love and relationships. The same style of writing has been used, which I hope you will find both interesting and humorous. Although we need to take all relationships seriously, it is also important to realise that we, as individuals, all have our faults and failings. Perhaps if we can take a 'sideways' look at these we can arrive at a better understanding of what makes ourselves, and others, turn out the way we are.

The reader will find the book written from the point of view of someone about to embark on a particular relationship, for the Chinese, like all wise people from history, realised that it was better to deal with a situation before it had a chance to turn sour. Barely a marriage would have taken place in ancient China without an astrologer being on hand to make certain that the couple in question were suited in terms of temperament and inclination.

Remember, though, despite astrology, our natures are not fixed in stone, and you might learn a lot about your existing relationships by looking carefully at the pages that follow. Perhaps if there are changes to be made these might spring from your own nature, rather than you naturally assuming that someone else has to make all the running. You can learn a great deal about yourself and others from both my books and I hope that the pages that lie ahead offer you a wry smile now and again, but also a short pause for thought.

Remember to use all the sections, until you have built up a true picture of the person concerned.

Of course, love and relationships formed a very real part of Chinese interest in the stars. They loved and lost, just as surely as we do today, and their explanation of human psychology and the way it had a bearing on relationships is as relevant now as it was all those thousands of years ago.

1900
1912
1924
1936
1948
1960
1972
1984
1996

The Rat

THE RAT IN LOVE

The Rat is a charmer. This is the first and most important fact to remember and is part of the reason that this particularly energetic and stimulating character is so easy to fall in love with. Here you will find the sort of love that is effusive, all giving and complete - for a while at least. However, to say that the Rat is incapable of being just a little fickle would be an untruth of the sort that occasionally slips from the mouth of the Rat itself.

All the same it is difficult to avoid responding to the sort of compliments that the Rat is inclined to bestow. These flow from this most endearing of Chinese signs like warm, liquid honey, are just as sweet and twice as potent as the strongest mead. When the Rat chooses to bestow its affections there is no holding back, so at least you cannot be left in any doubt at all as to how your potential partner feels about you. Nor is the Rat inclined to stand on ceremony, no matter where you happen to be at the time, so that if you are a particularly modest person yourself you could find this character a little overpowering right from the start.

Expect the Rat to be your champion in everything, but don't be surprised if he or she wants to fight all your battles on the way. It isn't that this individual fails to recognise that you are an individual in your own right, but merely that there is a combative instinct here that is second to none.

You would do well to make your own feelings known right from the start. At least that way the Rat can never say, further down the road, that you never expressed an opinion. There are occasions when this person can be a bully, though rarely if you stand up for yourself.

THE FEMALE RAT

Look out mankind, because it looks as though you have taken on something really special here! First of all you must remember that the Rat is generally considered to be a masculine sign of the Chinese zodiac. This means that, almost without exception, female Rats have all the drive, determination, potential for success and dynamism of any male counterpart. This makes it very important for the female Rat person to prove her capabilities and to exert her independence at almost every turn. The lady Rat will struggle long and hard to carve out a niche for herself in life, and will usually not relinquish it, even for the more dubious pleasures she sees in bringing up children. This is not to infer that family matters do not occur to Rats - indeed these individuals make splendid parents, though only on their own terms, which may not be yours.

Not only will you reasonably be expected to help with every aspect of housekeeping. On occasions you may be left with the lion's share of it. Meanwhile your Rat partner will be out jogging, socialising, wheeler-dealing and generally having a good time. When she comes home, stimulated by her brush with the outside world, there is not a more considerate partner in the length and breadth of the Chinese zoo.

You are not going to tame this free spirit, so there is really no point in trying. Yet paradoxically, many Rat women do really want to feel that they have a strong partner, who will cherish them and be of real support at times of difficulty.

Perhaps you don't have the patience of a saint and would find it difficult to play second fiddle to this individual, though the experience might be unforgettable.

THE MALE RAT

Let us be clear right from the start, that the Rat male is unlikely to get through a lifetime of potential relationships with members of the opposite sex, without a few accusations at some stage. The reasons are quite simple and relate in part to the very power of the personality in question.

Rat men are kind, attentive - up to a point - determined to follow their own path through life and tend to mix as well with members of their own sex as with the opposite gender. Male Rat types have charisma in abundance and a love of life that is so infectious, almost anyone will find it to be as contagious as a dose of Asian flu. When on the arm of this character you will feel a million dollars, especially in company, for your Rat companion cannot fail to give you a good time, or to make it evident to anyone who will listen, just how important you are to him. But this character is not destined for sainthood just yet and you can just as equally find the Rat male to be overpowering, too protective, somewhat jealous on occasions, and very much inclined to do what appeals to him, no matter how it goes down with you.

In a financial sense Rats usually manage to do well enough for themselves, and since they make such good parents, your Rat man will usually be willing to play with the children on their own level, and could make twice as much noise as they do into the bargain. Whether he will be around when the nappies need changing or when a feed is due in the middle of the night remains to be seen.

The male Rat can be boastful, though he can usually back up his arrogance with hard facts if necessary and is difficult to prove wrong in open argument.

THE RAT BEHIND
CLOSED DOORS

Perhaps you are the sort of person who quickly tires of a conventional love life, preferring, where possible, to ring the changes and to take a variety of lovers to your bed. Of course we all know how dangerous this can be these days, and it does have other disadvantages when compared with a more stable and permanent relationship. Well, you might have found just the right person if you have set your eyes in the direction of a Rat, because here you have the potential for change, but without going anywhere.

Remember first that the Rat is a great lover of variety, and can supply it as easily as he or she seeks it. This fact alone should pep up the quality of your sex life no end, though do not expect that its many possible twists and turns will be confined to the bedroom - dear me no. If your Rat partner is anywhere near typical you can expect to be approached indoors or out, up hill or down dale, at any possible hour of the day or night, and most likely of all when you least expect it. All of this you will be able to take on board and the only real problem begins, not when your Rat partner is demanding your sexual attention, but when he or she stops doing so. When this happens, alarm bells should start ringing in your brain and you need to leap into something seductive before the Rat quits your cage in favour of another.

All Rats, male or female, have a strong sex drive, though since this is a cerebral sign, you must remember that the Rat's sexual appetite can be as much mental as physical. For this reason, fantasy plays an important part in the life of the Rat, a fact which is as true in terms of sex as it is in any other sphere of life.

THE RAT AND CONSTANCY

So many relationships end up on the rocks these days, that it's natural to wonder, at the outset of any romantic prospect, what will be the chances of its surviving intact into the future. Since no individual is absolutely typical of any Chinese sign, this is certain to be a lottery, no matter what part of the animal zoo they come from. All the same, if gambling really isn't your thing at all, and if you are willing to forego interest in favour of relative stability, move away from the Rat enclosure as quickly as you can.

We've already seen that the Rat needs variety, and whether this can be supplied by one individual really depends on the way your own mind works and also on how much ingenuity you are capable of putting into the sort of varied life, sexual and otherwise, that your charming though sometimes unpredictable Rat requires. You simply cannot stand still and take things for granted in this relationship and will do far better if you make your mind up that life is an interesting journey, packed full of fascinating scenery. This is the way that Rats look at things, and although it might be selfish for anyone to expect their partner to view the world in the way that they do, the Rat just can't be any other way!

Investment pays great dividends here, for if you are willing to ring the changes, happy to be whatever is desired at the time, able to come to terms with changing mood patterns and capable of withstanding life in the eye of a hurricane sometimes, you could find yourself happier with the Rat than you ever considered yourself capable of being.

Most Rat people respond to kindness, concern and genuine love and are capable of showing all these, and more, in return.

牛

1901
1913
1925
1937
1949
1961
1973
1985
1997

IF I WANT YOURS

The Ox

THE OX IN LOVE

If 'What you see is what you get' could be said to be a truthful statement, it is never more so than in the case of the steady, trustworthy Ox. People born under this sign are hard-working, conscientious, determined and sometimes a little too serious for their own good. There is little room for illusion here and any tendency to expect this character to change its spots, rather more like a leopard than a steady plodding, cud-chewer, is likely to lead to disappointment.

However, it's the exception that proves any rule, and in this case the exception can be found in the way that the Ox responds to romance. True, you are not likely to find yourself on the receiving end of any glib chat line, and may not even be in a position to be chatted up by an Ox individual. Most of the time it would be someone else who would have to do the initial talking, for the Ox is as shy in romantic encounters as it is in almost any situation that is new to it.

It takes time then to win the heart of the Ox, though once you have done so it is unlikely that you would meet a more ardent or sincere lover no matter how hard you search. Part of the reason for this lies in the fact that there is a deeply earthy and sensual quality to the sign. Although the waters run deep here, they also run sure. The Ox individual feels everything at an intensity that many of the rest of us could seldom guess at, whilst many of us may offer a great display of our feelings, only to find ultimately that we may not have been quite as sincere as we had intended, this is seldom, if ever, the case with the steady, careful Ox.

In sexual terms the Ox is very highly charged, being as boisterous in the bedroom as it is quiet elsewhere.

THE FEMALE OX

Though shy and demure, the female Ox is friendly by nature and probably more approachable than her male counterpart. Relationships with the Ox often start in the realms of friendship in any case, and you really could not look for a better or more steadfast friend than you will find here. Once you are 'well in' with the Ox, unless you do something totally outrageous, the bargain is sealed for life. Miss Ox takes a great deal of provocation before she will lose her temper and will work hard to achieve her objectives in life, being more willing than almost any other sign to bear a common burden, and yet happiest of all it seems, to be working quietly alone.

Although this character may be uninspiring when confronted by much more gregarious types, the female Ox is seldom bored, often loves to sit and read, and, like the masculine Ox, probably loves wide open spaces beyond the confines of towns. The open countryside is the preferred resort of this sign, and so you may not find Miss Ox frequenting too many discos or propping up the bar in the pub. This is not to suggest that the Ox, male or female, is immune to the pleasures of life, but Ox people tend to socialise in the company of romantic partners, or good friends.

Although the female Ox may be good-looking, she is unlikely to be 'vivacious' in the truest sense of the word, and her sexuality is of a type that probably only shows itself to the favoured individual. If there is an apparent coolness here, don't be fooled by it, because the female Ox is well equipped, usually mentally and physically, to prove a lover of imagination and depth. It may take you a while to discover this fact, but this character has many hidden depths.

THE MALE OX

There is no bull in the Chinese Zodiac, and the more sedentary, plodding Ox comes about as close as it is possible to be for most purposes. But consider the reputation that the bull has, both for fertility and for ardour. Most people would be surprised to learn that Mr Ox comes very close to this idea, even if he achieves the feat from a considered and steady standpoint in life.

Mr Ox is a hard worker, and may spend long hours toiling away at the sort of tasks that would drive less patient types up the wall. He won't be the loudest member of any group, unless of course he has drunk a little more than is really good for him, and you might even find the male Ox to be shy in company he is not really certain about. Although he has a natural instinct to be protective, he tends to treat just about everyone, male or female, as an equal, and would rarely, if ever, stand on your right to have or express your own particular point of view.

Despite the above, Mr Ox is at his best in a settled sort of home and likes to know that his spouse will generally be at home to greet him. If the male Ox is not exactly chauvinistic he is certainly old-fashioned enough to recognise what he sees as being the differences between men and women. But he isn't always clever enough to know when you are getting your own way in any case and can quite easily be fooled into thinking that his wishes are being taken into account. This is a tried and tested method of dealing with the male Ox and one that is more or less certain to keep the peace.

There is no doubt that Mr Ox knows how to work hard and he is also excellent as a parent. One of the most practical of all Chinese signs!

THE OX BEHIND CLOSED DOORS

The Ox is a very singular sort of person, and not always easy to understand. Part of the trouble stems from the fact that there is an essential difference between the way the Ox shows itself to the world at large and the sort of impression that it offers to its nearest and dearest. The Ox is an earthy person at heart and is very practical by nature. Thus, to the world beyond your door, the Ox can appear to be very practical, quite matter-of-fact and even quite cool on occasions.

All of this is true of course, but does not represent the love-struck Ox, who turns out to be a very different kettle of fish altogether. The truth is that behind closed doors the Ox is deeply affectionate, sexually active and more than able to express the emotion that lies, not all that far, below that tough hide. The Ox has a great deal of love to offer, and displays this in all manner of ways. True, this individual may not be the most adventurous lover in the world, but he or she is definitely open to suggestion, is capable of physical feats that many others would find impossible to emulate and is a sensualist of the first order.

The Ox loves to lie for hours, alone or not, in a hot bath, is happy to enjoy a well cooked meal, and is just as pleased to do the cooking. A quiet evening at home with this character could turn into something much more when the wine flows freely and the Ox exhibits inhibitions that rapidly vaporise under the most intimate conditions. In the end it's not a case of wondering if the Ox can match your libido and emotional expectations. On the contrary it could be the other way round because when any Ox is willing to let down his or her hair, this person takes some keeping up with.

THE OX AND CONSTANCY

We all know that life is a lottery, and since there are many factors which have a bearing on any relationship, it is obviously wise to give considerable thought to any potential relationship. All the same, if you are the sort of person who worries about potential splits within personal encounters, practically before they have started, you could be onto a winner with the steady Ox.

When trouble threatens, and the pressures of everyday life put a strain on domestic harmony, the Ox usually manages to see the situation through without throwing a tantrum or running off to the nearest bar to seek liquid solace. Talking things through is a possibility, though it might be difficult to get the conversation started with an individual who tends to take things to heart at a deep level and who will often keep them right there. For this reason it is sometimes difficult to know what your potential Ox partner might actually be thinking, and it is worth a little gentle probing to break the ice. You will usually be rewarded, not by a string of vitriolic invective, but by a carefully reasoned appraisal of the situation, and a willingness to look at problems afresh.

Does all of this make the Ox into something of a saint? Not a bit of it but you can be fairly sure that this person will not be looking for a new entanglement the very minute that something goes wrong. The Ox is a one-to-one specialist who doesn't take well to extra-marital relationships and tends to stay close to home in the emotional stakes. It must be said that part of the reason for this is a lazy streak, for the Ox probably could not be bothered to go through all the preliminaries again and prefers to spend its evenings in the armchair.

虎

1902
1914
1926
1938
1950
1962
1974
1986
1998

NORTH POLE

The Tiger

THE TIGER IN LOVE

There is probably not a more enigmatic animal in the Chinese zoo than the Tiger and the way that any inhabitant of this cage is likely to act and react in any situation of love is almost totally dependent on circumstances. If the statement that 'the tiger walks alone' is accepted as a working adage, then the potential lover probably will not go far wrong.

'But hang on a minute', I hear the cry go up. 'My tiger partner is gregarious, sociable, kind and very affectionate!' True, but do you really know what is going on below the surface of the busy pool, for it is in the deepest recesses of the Tiger nature that the paradoxes are most pronounced. Tiger people are always looking for something, and they usually do not quite know what it is, which could create difficulties for any potential partner. For this reason, and a host of others, life with the Tiger individual could turn out to be far from easy unless you are a natural psychologist with the patience of a saint.

Having dealt with the point we can now dismiss it as being totally irrelevant in the majority of cases since, with the right mental and emotional stimulus, the Tiger is likely to prove the ideal lover. Not all of us want a totally predictable spouse and find great excitement amidst the cut and thrust of a Tiger-strewn environment. This individual is friendly, always ready for a laugh or an adventure and will dance the legs off you until dawn. He or she is usually intelligent and is adaptable enough to take many of your interests on board too. The Tiger hates routine, so you can expect variety in abundance, plus an inbuilt desire to keep the flames of passion burning brightly at all times.

THE FEMALE TIGER

Is there truly, in the length and breadth of the animal kingdom, a more beautiful or impressive animal than the Tiger? Well the Chinese sages of old were far from stupid in their choice of zodiac animals, so don't be surprised if Miss Tiger turns out to be a regular stunner. This might seem to be a little misleading however, since although this sign has more than its fair share of good-looking types, it is the reflection of the individual as a whole that proves to be the key to Tiger attraction.

The female Tiger is bright, bubbly, vivacious and interesting. You will usually know the minute she enters the room for she carries a certain 'something' that is tangible even behind your back. There is magnetism here, and the promise of a sexuality which might surprise even the most ardent Casanova. Miss Tiger is not at all afraid to let you know how she feels either and may take your breath away with the honesty of her approach and the confidence that seems to exude from every pore. If your instinctive reaction is to back away from a character who is so 'up front', then it might be sensible to listen to your inner mind right from the start, for the female Tiger is a formidable individual and is certainly not everyone's cup of tea.

Miss Tiger will never nag you or force you to do anything that goes against the grain, though it's a fair bet that you would find yourself doing whatever it is in any case, because she will have found the means to convince you that it was all your idea in the first place. She's a paradox wrapped in an enigma, because her appearance and attitudes often conflict with her genuine needs.

THE MALE TIGER

Look out all you females of whatever animal type, because once you catch a Tiger by the tail it might be difficult to let go again. This man is a charmer all right, and probably not at all what you expect him to be once you get under those oh so beautiful stripes. But from the word go he will keep you happy and seek in almost any way possible to show you that you are number one as far as he is concerned.

The only real problem comes when you have to make up your mind whether or not you want to believe the honeyed words that drip so readily from the tongue of this feline. To be fair, in the main the male Tiger is likely to be telling you the truth, that is if he has reason to be happy with his present lot. All in all this is not the most constant member of the Chinese animal fraternity, unless, of course, things are going his way.

Your Male Tiger may well turn out to be intellectual rather than physical, though this is an elegant beast, so he may well have more than his fair share of good looks too. In fact it might appear that you have found Prince Charming, Harrison Ford and Sean Connery all rolled into one, because to be quite honest this character appears to have everything. But all that glistens is not gold, so pin back your ears for the possible bad news.

The Tiger male is inclined to be very restless and as with the animal after which he is named, he often wants to hunt alone. He is definite in his opinions; as certain, in fact as he is that your choices are your own. In reality this might not be the case because he is so able to bring you round to his point of view. You would forgive this character time and time again, he's just that type.

THE TIGER BEHIND CLOSED DOORS

You really would expect this character, male or female, to be the best of the bunch as far as getting into a serious clinch is concerned. In reality you could be right, but it all depends on the circumstances. You must remember that your Tiger partner is an intellectual at heart, so that love-making is as much in the mind as it is in the bed. Get this aspect of things right and you are unlikely to be disappointed.

A Tiger partner will not usually bother you at times when you are not feeling especially romantic yourself, and you might even get a shock when you discover that he or she seems to be just as happy to sit up in bed and read a book. Be careful how you react to this situation however, because your Tiger is shrewd and may simply be goading you into making the first move - Clever eh?

This character has stamina, imagination, a good dexterity and usually the right sort of physique to make a more than passable lover. I cannot guarantee that his or her mind will always be in the bedroom with you, and if you are the sort who is troubled by fantasy, it might be best to leave the Tiger alone. However, the Tiger will happily take your own particular fantasies aboard too and at least you can be certain that once the antics are over you will find yourself in the company of someone who is especially interesting to talk to.

Many people would think that the Tiger is the ideal lover, especially in a sexual sense. There are few, if any, hang-ups here and a spontaneous approach that is refreshing, honest and often very funny. Speaking of humour, you can laugh at or with this person, as long as you are not too sensitive to take a little gentle ribbing in return.

THE TIGER AND CONSTANCY

If the Tiger is already aboard your ship of life, it might better to skip this page because it's a pretty safe bet that you did not opt for the most constant person in the world. Mind you, it all depends how you define the word and it also has far more to do with your own attitude in this case than it would with any other sign. The Tiger is a wild, free creature and you might have to let your cat out of the bag altogether in order to discover that you get back what you are most willing to let go.

The Tiger wants to be true to you in thought, word and deed, and if he or she fails to be so it is generally because there is some deep-seated unhappiness that needs to be dealt with. In certain situations the Tiger is the most patient person in the world, but he or she will only take so much of anything, and this is especially true in the case of nagging. There are always some sacrifices to be made if you want to carry perfection on your arm, and in the case of the Tiger this means allowing for a degree of flexibility over what you might consider to be faithfulness.

Of course it takes many people to make a world and even Tigers differ, one from another. But despite this there are benefits to be gained from your own actions. Try to be liberal, educated in your assessment of fidelity and willing to trust your Tiger and he or she is unlikely to let you down. Constrain the Tiger, show jealousy or be possessive, and you could be in for a very nasty shock one of these fine days.

An original person this, and probably quite unlike any other type you might meet. For the right partner the Tiger is well worth the effort, even if he or she is not always the easiest of people to come to terms with.

1903
1915
1927
1939
1951
1963
1975
1987
1999

The Rabbit

THE RABBIT IN LOVE

They say that still waters run deep, but never more so than in the case of the complicated, mysterious but often apparently serene Rabbit. This is a character who is difficult to get to know deeply and who will be much more willing to talk for hours on end about you than to spill the beans about his or her own innermost feelings. The Rabbit can wrap you up in a cocoon of affection and make you feel like the most important person in the world, a situation that may well suit you down the the the ground.

But here is a word of warning. It can be very appealing at first to have your every wish met and to be greeted on each and every occasion with the warmth you might expect after a six month absence. All the same, things might not appear to be quite so comfortable after a prolonged period of this treatment. Many types could start to feel smothered by love, and constrained to do what is expected, rather than what is personally desirable. If ever any animal sign was inclined to 'kill its joys with love' that creature is the affectionate, yielding, self-sacrificing Rabbit.

However, life is a balance, and there are great gains to be enjoyed from a Rabbit partner. He or she will be happy to wash your socks and to share all the chores of the house. They will fetch and carry, tend you when you are sick and look after the children better than a broody hen. The Rabbit will feed your ego, massage your pride and butter your bread, all at the same time. And as long as you are willing to pay the price, which is absolute fidelity and a willingness to be treated on occasion as if you were a precious china doll, all should be well indeed.

THE FEMALE RABBIT

This may well be the most deeply feminine of all Chinese animal signs, which in one way turns out to be a good thing, for the female Rabbit is often proud and happy to be just what she is. All the same too much of a good thing can be something of a problem and it is only fair to suggest that in the department of love the female Rabbit often has great difficulties. Whether the person in question is the one who creates the problems, or if their choice of partners is simply faulty, is difficult to tell.

The lady Rabbit is usually very sexy, often in a dark 'Earth Mother' sort of way. There is a basic magnetism here that is difficult to define and one that doesn't really depend on physical looks, though the female Rabbit is often very attractive indeed. She invariably fails to know exactly what it is she wants from life and can spend years looking, unsuccessfully, for the sort of relationship which she would find it impossible to define. Later in life the Rabbit might settle down a little but at base usually exudes a sort of 'divine discontent' that is impossible to define or understand.

Rabbits are not usually desperately career minded, and are great lovers of home life and family. Female Rabbits make good mothers, on occasions too good, and are at their best when surrounded by the people on whom they are willing to lavish so much attention.

The female Rabbit is often interested in metaphysical subjects and may also be a vegetarian. With so much to offer it might be difficult to turn down the female Rabbit, and for a whole host of reasons you probably would not dare to do so in any case. There is nothing more upsetting than a distraught Rabbit.

THE MALE RABBIT

Some people might suggest that the Rabbit is a better sign for a man these days than it is for a woman. The reasoning here is that a fair dose of female hormones makes for a more sensitive male and one who is always willing to see another point of view. In many respects this is true, but this fact can set up a whole series of difficulties as well. So many women who choose to live with the male Rabbit find that their own position in the family, and in life, is being eroded by a man who is so 'new' that he would make someone an extremely good wife.

Confidence is not the hallmark of this person, but you will find a sort of 'little boy lost' attitude that can be very appealing to some women, whilst being distinctly off-putting to others. The male Rabbit is capable of the deepest love imaginable and yet at the same time can become so eaten up with jealousy that he finds little else to consider. At base it seems that the driving force of masculinity does not always sit easy with the soul and intellect that is bestowed by this sign - and confusion can be the ultimate result.

It would be unfair to say that the male Rabbit is not worth the effort you would have to put in to understand him, because you might be just the right sort of person to benefit from the situation. In any case you could not find a more pleasant or giving type in the length and breadth of the zoo.

There is love and consideration on offer here that would dwarf that shown by almost any other animal type. You will have to remain faithful in thought, word, and deed though, because the Rabbit who feels thwarted can sulk most effectively. And fair or not, he can do so, and for weeks and weeks on end!

THE RABBIT BEHIND CLOSED DOORS

Do be careful, because you could be in for something of a shock here. You might have noticed that there seems to be something about your Rabbit pal that you can't quite come to terms with. It's a sort of sizzling below the surface and a latent sexuality that might be nothing more than your own overactive imagination. Well, it's likely to turn out that your intuition was correct, because the Rabbit has not gained its special reputation without justification.

It is to be hoped that you have the stamina to really make the most of the sexual side of this relationship, because the Rabbit has an appetite for personal physical contact that may not be bettered by many a more dynamic type. The best advice is to relinquish control of this side of the relationship. Although out there in the mainstream of life the Rabbit may sometimes be swamped by the requirements of life, behind the bedroom door this is certainly not the case. Both male and female Rabbits are equally adept as competent lovers and will do everything in their power to boost your ego and your libido.

There could be one or two strings attached however. Don't forget that romance plays an important part in the life of the Rabbit because although this character may be rampant at times, it is passion born out of genuine affection. Some Rabbit people give the impression of being promiscuous, but this is generally only a reflection of their need to find a stable, loving relationship.

Watch out for intensity and don't try to take anything for granted. This person is not always what he or she appears to be and so you could just be in for a shock if you fail to observe the rules.

THE RABBIT
AND CONSTANCY

This is the most difficult aspect of the Rabbit to deal with, and to understand. It isn't that the Rabbit actually wants to wander beyond its own burrow, merely that it has such a strong need for security that it often looks in strange places to find it. And it should be made plain from the very start that no truly contented bunny would ever dream of being unfaithful.

But how to keep your Rabbit pal happy and secure? Well this is the six million dollar question and it is going to take all your energy, cunning and resolve at times. You have to remember that this person was literally born to be insecure. Rabbit types are often quiet by nature and not at all inclined to say what they really think, so you might have to second-guess a great deal of what you know. Encourage truthfulness, but hold back on your own version of reality if you don't want to hurt the Rabbit's feelings.

Wherever possible you should tell the Rabbit just how much they mean to you, liberally sprinkling them with flowers, after-shave, or, since we are talking about the Rabbit, a new pan scrubber now and again. It doesn't matter how small the gesture is, because it is the act itself that is all-important. The Rabbit will never take these things for granted and will adore you like you've never been adored before. And at the end of this will your Rabbit partner remain faithful? The chances are that they will, and whatever happens they will not directly set out to hurt you. So genuinely kind is the Rabbit that he or she is always going to harm themselves the most in any case. The Rabbit character is basically insecure and no sign needs love and affection more than this one does. The returns might be well worth the effort.

1904
1916
1928
1940
1952
1964
1976
1988
2000

The
Dragon

THE DRAGON IN LOVE

It's a fact of life that, in fairy tales, Dragons tend to gobble people up. They may not want to, they probably never intended to, but people get eaten all the same. And this is what might happen to you in a relationship with a Dragon type, unless you are aware of the possibility and take the right precautions. The Dragon individual is dynamic, pushy, always on the go and inclined to be over-dramatic at times. The real person lies somewhere five floors below ground level and it will probably take you years to get that far, if you ever do at all.

Ignore the bluster, the raised voice, the assertive tendencies, be willing to wait and see. Remain patient, even when your Dragon is intent on taking on the world single-handed - they will probably win the battle in any case. In the meantime look towards the far less certain individual who sits at the heart of the driving Dragon, because that is the soul you want to fall in love with. Offer light sedatives when things get really exciting, enjoy the roller coaster ride when you can and always be on hand to sweep up the broken pieces when necessary.

Now if you can take all this on board, and a thousand other dynamic distractions too, you might just decide to fall in love with the Dragon. But hold tight to your knickers because this is going to be the journey of a lifetime. In return you will find a partner who is always interesting, rarely in the doldrums, and capable of loving you with a fierce intensity and who is great fun to have around.

The Dragon will run you ragged, prompt you, harass you and drive you to distraction. But you will love him or her with a passion that matches their own.

THE FEMALE DRAGON

This lady takes some tying down, and in any case would not take kindly to being restricted at all. It's probably fair to say right from the start that if Miss Dragon is anything like her sign, you would not be likely to get the better of her by being dynamic yourself. Female Dragons know what they want from life and are quite willing to use almost any sort of ammunition in order to get it.

The type of men who get on best with the female Dragon type are those whose needs exceed their own dynamic qualities because the Dragon always needs a cause and will usually support less pushy types than themselves. For these reasons it is unlikely that you would find two Dragons living together, for this would represent the most potentially explosive relationship imaginable. As in all situations however there are contradictions to the rule, but they are few and far between. Far better is the situation where the Dragon feels that there is something and someone to use as a focus for her own protective and supportive qualities, which are great.

Miss Dragon is warm personally, though sometimes a little intellectually aloof and in these post-feminist days might be a little out of fashion if she refuses to allow her more feminine qualities to shine through. At her best however she is the most refreshing person imaginable to live with, is always on the go and has energy to spare for everyone around her. She is unlikely to let you down, is always punctual and manages to burn the candle of life at both ends almost perpetually. The female Dragon hates routines of any sort and lives best in a spontaneous atmosphere of change, where excitement is a possibility too.

THE MALE DRAGON

If you want someone to rely on in a crisis, a man who will not crack under pressure and someone who is always different, interesting and dynamic, then Mr Dragon could well be for you. You should always remember though that the male Dragon is only really interested in being on top of the pile, is capable of being extremely possessive and jealous and is usually full of his own importance. Of course much of the more driving side of this sign overlays a person with much less self-confidence than might really seem to be the case. In order to realise this fact however, you must first get to know the real Dragon, and that isn't easy.

Everyone knows that Dragons breathe fire, though once you realise that in the case of Mr Dragon, there is more likely to be smoke than flames, you can easily start to ignore the inferno. This is, in fact the way most women learn to deal with the male Dragon and whilst others marvel at their ability to ride a whirlwind, the partner of this scaly time bomb usually carries on quite happily in her own sweet way.

Mr Dragon can be a contradictory chap because although he may push millions of pounds around the City every day, or build a sky-scraper single-handed, out of work he can be contented to potter about in the garden. The Dragon in his den could surprise a few folk, but take my word for it, a pipe and slippers are not unusual in the Dragon's lair. But that all comes further down the road, because the young Dragon always has something to prove and tends to show the fact at every hour of the day and night.

Not an easy sign to understand - but it might be interesting to try.

THE DRAGON BEHIND CLOSED DOORS

We have already seen that the Dragon can represent something very different from the fire-breathing monster of legend, once the driving needs of the day are put aside. All the same there is a personal pride and a 'me first' syndrome that must spill over into the more personal side of relationships. All Dragons like to think that they are the most desirable and sexually capable person ever to take breath, even if others sometimes find this to be overstating the case just a little.

It isn't just Mr Dragon who is proud of his sexual abilities because female Dragons can be tarred with the same brush. The basic problem is that anyone who sets themself up as being extra special in any way is also offering themself as a possible target to be shot down. The best Dragons are therefore the ones who have come to know their own natures well, who can laugh at their idiosyncrasies and then use what nature gave them to the best advantage.

Mr and Miss Dragon alike can be very possessive and display degrees of jealousy unknown to other Chinese signs. Any partner who feeds this tendency is in for a rough time, though ignoring it totally might also be quite difficult. It is best to take a middle path and to refuse to over-react either way. In this situation the Dragon will feel secure and offer the best of what he or she can be. This is really worth knowing and represents one of the best and most considerate lovers to be found anywhere.

The Dragon can be a good companion, a true and faithful partner and a tremendous support in times of trouble. That is if he or she is not out of the house and intent on making the next million!

THE DRAGON
AND CONSTANCY

Once you have taken the plunge and decided that you have the fortitude and stamina to take on a Dragon partner, can you be at all certain that this individual will still be around in a few month time, let alone a few years? Well the simple answer to this question is: It really depends on you.

This might seem like refusing to be specific, and in a way it is. Like many of the more dynamic Chinese signs, that of the Dragon infers a tendency towards restlessness, and this is probably the only real factor that would make the Dragon inclined to seek fresh fields and pastures new. At the same time the Dragon is something of a paradox because he or she really does need a degree of stability as far as home life is concerned. Add to this the fact that the Dragon always has to be in charge, and you have a formidable combination of requirements.

This is where you come in as a partner. If you have the ability to provide a stable environment which is based on genuine love and a high degree of admiration, feigned or otherwise, you could be on the way to success. The Dragon is a thinker and will not readily throw up a potentially good life just for the sake of taking a chance. Since this individual also cares about money, a joint bank account could also be a good idea.

It all sounds terribly cynical, but if you want to keep a Dragon returning time after time to the same cave, and to leave all the other damsels or knights in shining armour alone, it is probably along these lines that you will have to think. But despite all of this, the Dragon is, in any case, the easiest individual to love - for a certain sort of person.

1905
1917
1929
1941
1953
1965
1977
1989
2001

The Snake

THE SNAKE IN LOVE

I used to wonder if the Chinese sages of old really had things right in naming this sign the Snake. After all, people born under this sign are not sly, rarely liable to strike out nor can be seen as particularly dangerous types. But as always, I was wrong and the ancient astrologers were right.

The Snake is patient, happy to work at things for a considerable time to get them right, but at the same time is capable of being extremely lazy. All snakes, human or otherwise, are fond of luxury and would much rather lie around in the sun than actually do anything concrete. Snake people are definite sensualists, in terms of food, drink, clothing, personal adornment and, of course, sex. The average Snake could well grow a little portly around the middle unless they get sufficient exercise, though this state of affairs may well suit them.

In return for your love you will find genuine devotion, a commitment to yourself and the family and a willingness to work diligently to build a better life day by day. You might not always have the excitement you need, though it is easy to fall in line with the Snake mentality and to become hypnotised by that warm smile and comfortable attitude to life. You may easily wake to the dawn of each new day, thanking your lucky stars that your Snake is generally even-tempered, always reliable and usually willing to do what they can to make you even happier.

The Snake person can be rather stubborn on occasions, and if you have the same tendencies this could cause a little friction, though all in all, and if you are flexible, you may never regret setting up home with the likeable, comfortable Snake.

THE FEMALE SNAKE

If it is possible for a person to be all things to all men, it is likely to be the female Snake who comes closest to this adage. She has at her disposal most of the qualities that any self-respecting man would also respect in a potential partner. The female Snake is warm, considerate, highly charged sexually and very fond of home and family. She usually loves to cook good food and is happy to be a home-maker, at the same time often holding down a successful career.

Your lady Snake will generally be busy, doing this or that, though she is not shy of spoiling herself a little too. She loves to sit for ages in a hot bath and would definitely be a beach reptile on holiday in the sun. She could sometimes profess herself to be rather dull, and yet you would probably disagree with her opinion, for she has a good understanding of life, is invariably willing to listen to what you have to say and will rarely make excessive demands.

Under this charming exterior she has a tendency towards being quite stubborn if she is continually crossed and a reticence to relinquish control over anything that she thinks belongs exclusively to her. She can be something of a materialist, though is unlikely to be selfish over possessions and gets the greatest kick out of sharing them with the chosen few. You would rarely find yourself at odds with the female Snake, because in the main she does not care for arguments. All the same she knows how to get her own way if it is really necessary and is not beyond some subterfuge if that is what it takes to get on.

Give and take from your direction will be appreciated and would make life more than happy in the fullness of time.

THE MALE SNAKE

This is a character who generally knows what he wants from life, and from relationships. From the word go it must be understood that he might not appear to be the most dynamic sort of person you will ever meet, though he does have much going for him in the reliability stakes. The male Snake is often quiet, gets on with things in his own sweet way and is generally good around the house in a practical manner. He may not seek too much excitement in his life, but he does know how to enjoy himself and will always put his family first.

If this sounds to be a dull sort of person, the truth is that it really depends on you. It would be fair to say that the Snake male who is left entirely to his own devices could turn into something of a domestic machine, which is why you will have to insist that the changes are rung on a regular basis. Under these circumstances the Snake chap will adapt easily, travel willingly and join in almost any sort of fun.

Snake men often seek to keep themselves fit, which is just as well because they are inclined to put on a little weight. They can be very artistic, full of abilities for making money and work well for themselves. Interests can be varied, but number one on the list is likely to be you. Your Snake man will wash the dishes, hoover the carpet and make the beds. When you are ill he will look after you and when you are not he can turn out to be a surprisingly interesting sort of lover.

One word of caution however. Because Snake men are inclined to be a little lazy it would be better not to buy him a pair of slippers for Christmas. Make it a surfboard instead. And you might decide to get rid of the television while you are about it!

THE SNAKE BEHIND CLOSED DOORS

Snakes love luxury, there is no denying this fact. And this may be part of the reason why few of them will have relished sexual encounters in the back of the car or down some leafy, but grubby, lovers lane. The best place for a Snake individual to give of their best sexually is between satin sheets, in some perfumed paradise of pillows. This would certainly be more or less guaranteed to get the best out of any Snake and might ensure life-long devotion to whoever organised this feast of sensual delights.

In most circumstances the Snake must be carefully aroused in order to get the most out of any deeply personal encounter. This is not a 'Wham, bam, thankyou Ma'am' type at all and needs love to be part of the scenario in order to be truly relaxed and lacking in any sort of inhibition. To counter this the Snake has great fortitude and stamina, a good imagination and a body that, though it may weigh a pound or two over the odds, was clearly made for sex. But happiness is the key and you will not get anywhere near the best out of your Snake partner unless he or she is relaxed, and enjoying life in the way that only Snake people can.

Love and sex go hand in hand in the case of this sign, so promiscuity is probably not likely. This means that you may well be the first to arouse your Snake partner. Don't worry, Snakes can learn very quickly when they wish and the promise of paradise that you see in their eyes is easily turned into a reality.

This individual could take you to heights you never dreamed about, but it's certain to take a little effort on your part. The mental and physical exercise could do you good.

THE SNAKE AND CONSTANCY

Although the Snake individual is probably the most loyal person in the whole Chinese zoo, this very fact can turn itself into a real problem if it isn't looked at carefully, right from the very start. The problem is that the Snake is also the easiest person in the world to take for granted and he or she is usually such a treasure that there will always be someone about who is willing to take your place if you allow them to do so.

Any object of inestimable worth needs to be looked after carefully and this is true with people too. It is especially true in the case of the Snake. It won't be hard to keep this individual locked into the relationship, and every little exercise on your part promises to pay so many dividends that nothing should be too much trouble.

The Snake represents a bottomless well into which you can keep throwing love, concern and devotion for ever. In return, the water will only become sweeter and sweeter with every passing day.

Watch out for the man or woman next door. They have seen your Snake partner in action and since the Snake does not like to wander all that far, any extra-marital happening may not be too far from your own doorstep. However, if things do get to this stage it is likely to be because you have not put in sufficient effort yourself. Once you do lose a Snake, it is likely to be for good, which will leave you without a lover and mean that you also have to do more housework than before.

Avoid routines, keep things interesting and maintain your effort. The returns are more than worthwhile and you could find yourself part of an ideal relationship that the whole world would envy.

1906
1918
1930
1942
1954
1966
1978
1990
2002

The Horse

THE HORSE IN LOVE

Make certain that your feet are firmly planted on the ground, and that you have something sturdy to hold onto because there is a tornado on the way. The Horse person is one of the most charming and accommodating types that you could ever wish to meet, yet wherever they are the world is in turmoil and change batters everyone. Not that this is an entirely bad thing, since to many people variety is the spice of life. The Horse certainly thinks so, that is if any thought actually goes into the process at all.

As a lover the Horse is kind and considerate, and will pay you the most eloquent compliments until the cows come home. You will feel like the most important person in the world and the boost to your ego is not at all transitory, even if the presence of the Horse actually is. The main problem might be that you want more of the same and when you turn round to find it, your elusive Horse has galloped off to do something else completely. Wait patiently and sometime later, back he or she comes, and offers the next dose of elixir.

You cannot help loving the Horse, because there is nothing malicious or nasty about this person. Some people call the Horse shallow, but in reality this is not true. The Horse means everything that he or she says, but is capable of the same intensity in a thousand other directions too. If this fact takes the shine off the things that have been said to you, then you don't really understand the way that the Horse type functions.

All in all you could do a lot worse. Horses are usually successful, always entertaining, rarely down and invariably anxious to live life to the full. As long as you are the same, there should be no problem.

THE FEMALE HORSE

This lady might seem well beyond the reach of any mere mortal when viewed from a distance and yet she is one of the most approachable people you could possibly imagine. She probably has a million acquaintances, even if close personal friends are fewer in number. You will almost certainly meet her at a party, or some other social gathering, and she won't be sitting alone in a corner. The female Horse is vivacious, sexy, interesting, informative, intelligent and apparently wise. She can sort out the combined problems of the world in a moment, but may never be able to resolve fully the personal problems that surround her as an individual.

She lives a crowded life, and no matter how much she strives to clear her diary of appointments, more come in all the time to demand her attention. Because of this the female Horse is inclined to tire herself out, so that only a full day in bed can restore her capacity for life, which begins again the moment she has left the bedroom. An astrologer can become exhausted simply writing about the Horse and the female of the species is no less tiring than her male counterpart.

The lady Horse has a depth of charm and a natural sparkle that is attractive to almost all members of the opposite sex. She can work hard, play hard and love hard. This individual can turn the world upside down and your own life inside out. She is not malicious but is capable of persuading you that black is white if she chooses to do so. But at the end of it all you may find a love here that is without parallel. Kindness is the hallmark of the sign - and what more could you ask? Perhaps only a few minutes peace and quiet, which is not always that easy to find!

THE MALE HORSE

I am quite of the opinion that Romeo, in Shakespeare's famous play about the star-crossed lovers, was a Horse. His capacity for love at first sight, his passion, eloquence and impetuosity are all typical of the Horse. He enters the play deeply in love with one woman, and within a short time is so fond of Juliet that he is willing to give up fortune, fame and even his very life. And all this for the sake of a young woman who was a stranger to him just a few hours before. The fact that Juliet responds in the way that she does only goes to show how persuasive the male Horse is capable of being.

Don't run away with the idea that the Horse fella is fickle though, even though this is what other people will try to tell you. He will be equally serious about each romantic attachment he is ever likely to have. The trouble is that there tend to quite a few of them, and sometimes more than one at once!

If you can manage to hold onto your male Horse for an entire lifetime you will never be without interest, will often be staggered at his capacity to 'know' almost anything and will probably be enchanted by his general appeal. On the less fortunate side you may tire of his constant motion, be infuriated by his apparent flirtations and become fatigued by his inevitable ups and downs. Life is a balance and it is up to you to decide if you can cope with the negatives, in order to benefit from the positives. You can be certain that life will be fascinating and that the word 'boredom' will never invade your personal dictionary. If this sounds good, take a deep breath and plunge into the waves of love. It is only to be hoped that you can swim.

THE HORSE BEHIND CLOSED DOORS

Let us get one thing clear right from the start. The Horse has what amounts to the best imagination of any zodiac sign. Whether or not you choose to turn this fact to your advantage is really up to you. As with all situations, there are positives and negatives to be considered.

It is fair to say, that no matter how much passion your Horse mate shows in personal situations, there could be times when you doubt that his or her mind is firmly fixed on present events. But fantasy is so much a part of the way the Horse thinks, a little cunning on your part is all that is needed. What it comes down to, is feeding and directing the fantasy, rather than turning away from it.

It isn't everyone's cup of tea to dress in kinky clothes or to use other aids to personal pleasure, and if you are reticent in this department, perhaps the Horse is not the ideal partner for you. There are many occasions, if you have the same ability to communicate that the Horse does, when words alone may be enough. And perhaps the greatest advantage of all is that your own needs will be scrupulously taken care of, because a Horse partner will move mountains to be anything that your heart desires.

Some people would see this as the best recipe for success in a sexual sense and it is true that a wise individual can make much out of the Horse intelligence and imagination. Duration might be something different and it really depends on whether your Horse mate has anything else to do at the time.

Try to look on the bright side. You might get up in the morning and discover, to your great surprise, that the washing up has been done too!

THE HORSE AND CONSTANCY

Oh dear, this is not the best department for the Horse, and it would be unfair to suggest that you can expect life-long devotion from your Horse partner, unless you take the necessary precautions yourself to make certain that it is so. Any relationship is a two-way street and this is especially true in the equine department of the Chinese zoo.

But let us get one thing clear. The Horse really wants to be faithful and suffers from terrible guilt if things don't turn out this way. And perhaps this is unnecessary. As long as you can manage to keep the compliments flowing, the ideas coming and the emotional temperature up in the 80s, you have probably captured the Horse for life. If you can be all things to all people, or at least to one wayward mare or stallion, then not only will you have a contented life, but an extremely happy one. The Horse wants to adore you forever and if you make the situation possible, that will be the almost certain result.

You will go through all sorts of ups and downs, and may never be absolutely certain that things will look quite the same tomorrow as they do today, but you will never be bored and should experience much fun on the way.

Meanwhile the Horse will prove to be a good, if somewhat anarchistic parent, and will help you with almost any chore around the house, that is if they are around to do so. Take heart, this character is the easiest person in the whole world to love and very difficult to bear a grudge against.

If you are clever, it's hearts and flowers all the way and yet there can be a down-side too. No sign in the Chinese zodiac responds more to the atmosphere within which it is living than does the Horse.

1907
1919
1931
1943
1955
1967
1979
1991
2003

The Goat

THE GOAT IN LOVE

The Goat is a shy animal, a fact that is also quite obvious in most people born under this Chinese sign. For some reason this fact puts a number of people off trying to strike up a deep relationship with the sign. This could worry the Goat a little and help to induce the nervy side of the Goat nature, which is quite pronounced in any case.

Once the barriers are down, this is an affable, warm and very genuine character, who possesses courage, good organising abilities and a practical common sense that is second to none. The Goat is a deep sensualist and being emotionally warm, delights in being loved absolutely. Some people would say that the Goat can be rather too serious for his or her own good, but all members of the flock are likely to be very family minded, and devoted to those for whom they show a deep concern.

The Goat is not likely to make a first move romantically, and may even seem cool until you get to know their character better. This is not a one-night stand and it is fair to suggest that you gain more from a relationship with the Goat as time goes by. The effort you put in is directly mirrored back at you however, and there never was a better investment in time and devotion than this one.

Goats are often successful in a material sense, usually by dint of perseverance. A quiet, pleasant and usually delightful exterior overlays the more competent qualities that lie beneath. The Goat person is famous for his or her warm smile and pleasant personality and is usually happy to settle for one relationship at a time, which is often also for life. Certainly a steady sign, that of the Goat.

THE FEMALE GOAT

Many people would think that this is the ideal sign for a woman, and a potential romantic partner to have, though of course it's all a matter of your own point of view. It is true to say that the lady Goat is warm, kind, sincere, deeply romantic and the ideal home-maker. She is also a good mother, a sterling friend and a very special sort of person generally. What might go along with all of this however is a tendency to worry too much about the kids, an obsession with keeping the home spotless, and the willing ignorance of her own lot in life for the sake of others.

The female Goat is at her best in some caring profession, which would allow her natural caring tendencies to be projected into practical and possibly lucrative directions. The female Goat will always be on hand to wash a cut knee, mop a fevered brow and calm a troubled mind, and to some this makes her just too good to be true. She will take any amount of stress, though will eventually break out and prove why she was called the Goat in the first place. If you ever do manage to get her to the stage of losing her temper, then woe betide you! The Goat is a great fighter and the females of the species are included.

You won't find her too demanding, though you might not find her to be especially passionate either, since her idea of romance is just that and may not include a fondness for prolonged romps of the sort that other signs would take for granted.

Miss Goat tends to be very faithful and especially giving. She probably needs to lighten up a little however and you might be just the person to help her do so, as long as you are patient in the way you go about it.

THE MALE GOAT

The male Goat is often a natural born home-maker, is a warm and affectionate partner and a particularly good friend. You will enjoy his company under most circumstances and should find him to be the greatest 'mate' that you could possibly have. Maintaining the status quo is always easy with the male Goat around, though actually changing things significantly might be more difficult.

If it is Indiana Jones that you are looking for, the male Goat may not be for you, though he is fond of travel and would relish the sort of journey which is 'different' in some way. All the same, he does like to be at home much of the time, and so can alternate between contentment and restlessness.

Passion, in the strict sense of the word, may not be Mr Goat's stock-in-trade, and you do need to put a bomb under his rear end sometimes if you want to get the best out of his potential. In a deeply personal sense he has what it takes to keep you happy, but you might have to do some of the initial running and will need to ring the changes in order to keep things fresh and alive.

Personality is not something that is naturally inherent to the male Goat, though those who would assert this probably do not know him as well as they might. You could find him to be just the right sort of person to spend the rest of your life with and, once he has made up his mind, he could be around for good.

Mr Goat is a good worker, adores his family and is probably never going to be 'one of the boys', so chances are you will know where to find him most of the time. He needs to lighten up a little and maybe you can help him.

THE GOAT BEHIND CLOSED DOORS

We have already seen that all Goats, both male and female, are deeply romantic. Now 'romance' is a strange word and means different things to different people. If you recognise it as deep and continued response to your own sexual overtures, you might be reading the wrong dictionary as far as the Goat is concerned. This is not to infer that the Goat has no sexual passion - dear me no! But to realise it to the full you must know the person very well and also have an idea about how to get the best out of the potential.

All Goats need to feel very secure and nobody would tempt a Goat partner by keeping him or her guessing. Unlike many signs, the mind of the Goat tends to be focused on an immediate partner, so that the Goat is neither promiscuous or a particular student of fantasy.

It's fair to say that things could become rather 'samey' if you leave the whole situation to the Goat, so it is important to know how to pep up a flagging sexual life, though without making the situation so obvious that you cause the Goat to worry. If you are wise, the answers should be obvious to you, and you will find a partner who can love you with a sustained passion that you barely dreamed of.

But even aside from this, and when the bed sheets are back in place, the Goat will always be your best friend, and it's likely that you will want to spend more time with him or her than with any other living soul.

Those who have this sort of a relationship may be the luckiest people of all and so sex can take an important but not an overriding place. Like most things, it slots sensibly into a balanced whole.

THE GOAT AND CONSTANCY

Everything about the Goat tends to lead one to believe that here we have a personality who was built for fidelity. In fact, in the main, this is true. However, this does not mean that you have a natural reason to take your Goat for granted, because as surely as a worm can turn, the constant Goat can as well. The difficulty is that you may not know what is happening to your relationship until you wake up one day to find that it is too late. A real problem is that it is so easy to take the Goat individual for granted.

Day after day, year after year, the Goat soldiers on in his or her own steady way, whilst you benefit from the natural charity of this most endearing person. But did you make a fuss over your Goat's birthday, probably arranging a surprise party? How often do you actually display your own emotions and utter those three little words that are so very important to the happiness of this individual? If you are living with a Goat and have no satisfactory answer to these questions, perhaps this is the time to start putting things right.

The simplest of responses would be enough to secure the affection of the Goat and to make your partner feel like the most important person in the world. Once you achieve this, the rest is easy, because the Goat genuinely does want to love you forever and in an exclusive way.

Don't forget that you are living with a beautiful and giving individual and that you would walk a long journey before you would find a better soul mate. Your efforts will pay off in terms of a happy life and a partner who tries even harder on your behalf. If there is much more than this that any reasonable person could require, is hard to imagine what.

1908
1920
1932
1944
1956
1968
1980
1992
2004

The Monkey

THE MONKEY IN LOVE

Here we have an individual who is full of charm, character and individuality. It would be fair to suggest that the Monkey is capable of being strong willed and even headstrong on occasions, so that nobody who is also a very dominant type would be likely to last long with this type. Male and female Monkeys alike know what they want from life and have the ability to go out and get it. You need to climb out of bed very early in the morning to get one over on the Monkey, who always seems to know what you are thinking and is invariably one step ahead of you.

The Monkey is extremely loyal, both as a friend and a lover. There is a certain charm here, together with a sunny disposition and a natural warmth that makes the Monkey fun to be with, always interesting and definitely a charmer. Here we have a person who is capable of working hard and playing hard, and whose interest in life extends to almost any subject. The Monkey likes to spoil itself when work is out of the way, though being energetic, this could easily mean a night out on the town. Being naturally truthful, the Monkey could well tell you things about yourself that you are not really certain you want to know. They probably impart this knowledge in a fairly matter-of-fact way though and are quite capable of accepting your truths concerning them.

Routines are not popular with the Monkey, who wants to ring the changes as often as possible. This individual loves to travel, adores the sunshine and is capable of being a monarch amongst humanity. A regal creature this, even if both male and female Monkeys keep you laughing from morning until night.

THE FEMALE MONKEY

Miss Monkey can be a real chatterbox, but don't be fooled because she is certainly no empty-headed bimbo. She possesses charm, in addition to a ready tongue, and in any case she is not a gossip and always knows what she is talking about. In her work she can be a solo hunter, no matter how much she enjoys being around other people too. The female Monkey is generally very successful and might be employed in some capacity that brings her into contact with selling a service or a commodity. She does not suffer fools gladly, either in the office or the bedroom, but has a tremendous sense of fun and will always beat you to the punchline of any joke.

Many men would find Miss Monkey to be something of a puzzle because on the one hand she is capable of being very independent and yet seems to need so much confidence-building in other directions. Often she seems lost inside herself emotionally and could probably appear to be fickle as a result. The truth is rather different because the Monkey is basically a loyal person and will reward fidelity with deep affection, a strong sexual drive and good executive ability, even at home.

Female Monkeys can be very attractive to look at, but in any case have such a magnetic personality that the word 'plain' really does not apply to this individual at all.

Tied down, or fettered by convention, Miss Monkey visibly wilts and does need constant bolstering of her ego in order to give of her best. She is not always the easiest of people to live with and yet the rewards are many for the patient and attentive partner.

Miss Monkey is a handful - but what a handful she turns out to be!

THE MALE MONKEY

Here we have a fairly dynamic sort of chap and someone who is generally very happy to be exactly what nature made him. If this means that there is a little arrogance present, then that is part of the price that must be paid for such dynamism. This does not necessarily mean that the male Monkey is a bore to be with or that you will tire of his constant assurance that he knows what he is doing.

The Monkey man has a disarming ability to put across his point of view in a way that is very acceptable and not at all pushy. There are occasions when you will wonder, with hindsight, how you were so easily swayed, though you will soon get used to the fact.

The male Monkey is usually successful, has a good executive ability at work and rarely has to get his hands dirty in order to earn a good living, not that to do so would bother him in the slightest. Many 'self-made men' come from this sign, but they usually retain a much higher degree of humility than many people would under such circumstances and are charmers through and through.

Believing that they were cut out to do something special with their lives, Monkey males are often generous to a fault and especially good with the needy.

Your needs will usually be met by this character, though he might expect you to come round to his point of view in most things, even if he talks constantly about equality. Monkey types are often quite sexy, in an imperious sort of way, and love to hand out presents and compliments in equal quantity. This man could be quite sporty, so if you hate football - ask him before the relationship gets started!

THE MONKEY BEHIND CLOSED DOORS

Monkeys, male and female alike, do need to have and retain a fairly good opinion of themselves and this of course applies just as much to their sexual abilities as it does to any other facet of their nature. In the case of the very dynamic Monkey types, this can be something of a problem, creating a potential sexual athlete of the sort that can be quite boring. Not that this is inevitable.

For starters most Monkeys tend to have a fairly balanced view of themselves and the world and are quite capable of laughing at their own idiosyncrasies. The secret is to smile when they do, but never to laugh at anything they do behind the closed bedroom door.

Large egos are often more susceptible to being dented than smaller examples and this is certainly the case with the Monkey. It is also fair to say that some of the most positive and successful types also need to be led around by the hand in areas that they are less familiar with. A Monkey who is inexperienced sexually is likely to try and make up for the fact with bluster and bragging. Take heart however, because this is not the genuine person you are dealing with and it is only a matter of time before experience brings confidence. In turn, confidence allows consideration and understanding, which abound with this sign.

The Monkey has great staying power and an explosive potential with regard to all aspects of life, so you could find interesting times ahead once any initial hitches are out of the way. It is best to keep all sexual encounters with this individual as light-hearted as possible and to make certain that things do not become too routine.

THE MONKEY
AND CONSTANCY

Here we may be in the realms of potential difficulties, especially in the case of a Monkey type who does not feel that life is going quite the way they might really wish. When things are either dull or less than successful, the Monkey can turn to those aspects through which it feels it is capable of 'quality' expression. Sex is one of the areas. In short, the Monkey needs to feel happy and fulfilled with his or her life as a whole if the more personal aspect of relationships is to be harmonious.

You can help no end with this regard because nobody responds better to being preened and praised than the Monkey does. This will not only improve your personal life, but could urge the Monkey on to greater efforts that lead to yet more success.

No sign of the Chinese zodiac requires a firmer base from which to work than the Monkey does, for without it here we have a sad character indeed. You have the responsibility of making the Monkey feel really important, both inside and outside of your relationship, so you need to help with career matters too and should always be on hand to offer words of encouragement.

All of this takes a good deal of effort, though you should find the results to be more than worthwhile. For your pains you will have a partner who is rarely, if ever, inclined to wander, and someone who will keep their sights firmly fixed upon you. As long as you remember that there is no end to this process, you should find that your Monkey is attentive, constant and always ready to help you just as much in return. It's a mixed bag for certain, though usually a very interesting one.

1909
1921
1933
1945
1957
1969
1981
1993
2005

The Rooster

THE ROOSTER IN LOVE

Very few creatures in the Chinese menagerie are capable of the depth of love and affection that is forthcoming from the Rooster. Love is an art form to this person and includes a degree of concern, care and worry that some others may even find to be rather stifling. The Rooster is a natural home-maker but can go over the top in this direction, providing the sort of neat and tidy cocoon that is, quite frankly, not always especially comfortable. The secret is to turn the Rooster's concern away from the state of the covers on the three-piece suite and towards matters beyond the front door, or perhaps behind the one that guards the bedroom.

Some individuals would call the Rooster emotionally cold, but this is a misrepresentation of the situation. Many people show their affection with hearts and flowers, whilst others are very good at making cakes. The Rooster often falls into the latter category and as a result has gained itself a rather dubious reputation in some quarters. The Rooster does have a keen intellect and needs to be forced down channels that might not initially be of its own choosing. The more this overgrown chicken sees of the world outside, the greater will be its desire to make the best use of what is on offer.

The Rooster is incredibly good at earning a living and gives of its best in both a practical and a theoretical sense in the company of others. These individuals are chatty, kind, persevering but sometimes just a little over fussy. Confidence is not the hallmark of the sign and Rooster people are rarely as settled emotionally as they would like to give the impression of being. Most people like the Rooster, and some absolutely adore it. Which one are you?

THE FEMALE ROOSTER

The Chinese sage of old, who apportioned animal signs to all the differing zodiac signs, really seem to have hit the nail on the head in the case of the Rooster. I don't wish to sound insulting, but the extremes of this sign, and especially the archetype female Roosters, can even look like hens on occasion. The worst of the breed strut and cluck about, always broody and inclined to want to keep every chicken in the nest for as long as possible. Some Roosters will go to any length to keep their families intact and might well drive the offspring away at the first possible opportunity.

Fortunately very few of us are exactly like our animal year sign, though there is always a degree of truth in them and in the case of the Rooster, the less desirable traits really do need to be worked on. As a compensation, and a great one at that, the lady Rooster is as kind as the day is long, very capable, extremely successful at anything she undertakes and is a perfect social hostess. She is unlikely to be interested in liberation, mainly because she is already in charge in any case, even though she would fight tooth and nail to deny the fact. Miss Rooster is careful, calculating and confident in those jobs and activities that she really understands. You will often find her with her head in a book and she has a lively imagination.

This sign is not everyone's cup of tea, but there are literally millions of people in the world who live lovingly and amicably with female Roosters.

Rooster lovers wish for nothing more than what they already have and are quite happy to be what others would call 'henpecked'! Of course it's not true. I know because a lady Rooster told me it wasn't!

THE MALE ROOSTER

The male Rooster is not really the sort of fowl that you would have expected to see winning its spurs in a medieval cockpit. In fact there does not appear to be anything very combative about the male Rooster at all, though that does not prevent him from being immensely successful all the same. In the main he is a not too confident type who often talks a lot and frequently seems to be a bag of nerves. You might feel sorry for him on this account and yet, underneath, he is as tough as old boots. This is the man who you would discover waiting in the doctor's surgery, convinced that he has every disease under the sun and yet about to celebrate his 102nd birthday!

The male Rooster has a soft spot for just about everyone, loves women and children especially and is universally kind to animals, except the ones he manages to cook most successfully when he is not building a garage or refurbishing the caravan. This character is always on the go and is very practical.

If you want to be cast up on a desert island with the perfect mate, take the male Rooster along to be your Man Friday. He doesn't pretend to know everything about everything - he really does!

Create a happy atmosphere for Mr Rooster and he will do all in his power to make you happy in return. Buy him a new set of carpentry tools for Christmas and he will love you forever. The male Rooster loves to make lists, probably collects stamps and may once have been a train-spotter to boot!

Despite all this he is charming, loving, kind, attentive and protective to a fault. He will tell you sincerely that you are the most wonderful person that he has ever met. Don't knock it - he is probably trying to be sincere.

THE ROOSTER BEHIND CLOSED DOORS

Now let's be fair about this. You are going to come across a significant number of Chinese astrologers who will tell you that the Rooster is not over-endowed with imagination in a personal sense. To a certain extent this has to be true, but this does not account for what amounts to the best stamina of almost any sign and a sexual appetite that might truly surprise any potential partner.

It isn't always easy to judge any individual on the grounds of first impressions and this is certainly true in the person of the Rooster, who in any case has far more drive and determination than might seem to be the case at first.

An important fact here is the retention of a partner who really understands what makes this rather 'steady' bird tick. There needs to be constant mental as well as physical stimulation and a few choice suggestions at the right time might do more to perk up life in the chicken coop than anything.

In all things it is necessary to realise that the Rooster is a lover of consistency - which might be the best recipe for a boring sex life than just about any other blessing or fault. It is up to you to prove to your Rooster that variety is the spice of life.

Since Roosters are often very fond of reading matter of one sort or another, the addition of the right sort of books to your personal life could be a distinct advantage, plus the ability on your part to play out a temporary role if you have to.

If this advice is heeded on the part of any would-be partner of a typical Rooster, a red-hot, happy and quite stimulating private life is the likely result.

THE ROOSTER AND CONSTANCY

Roosters tend to have very big feet, and prising them out from under any table is not going to be easy, so this relationship, once started, probably could not be forced apart with a crowbar. Of course there have to be exceptions to any rule and there may well be Roosters about who would fly the coop at the drop of a hat - or some other garment of clothing, though this astrologer is certainly not familiar with any of them.

The Rooster is many things. Reliable, consistent, cautious, affable and even noisy on occasions. However, in this list the word 'unfaithful' is not likely to appear. Part of the reason for this might be that the Rooster takes such care in making choices in the first place, the majority of them choose wisely and usually for life. Unfortunately in some cases this can lead to tedium and even boredom on the part of a spouse so that the Rooster is much more likely to be 'left' than to 'leave'. Diversions are important, even if they are only in the mind, because they keep relationships alive and fresh. Once again this is down to you as the Rooster's closest friend and lover.

It would be cruel to tease the Rooster for his or her steady ways, but a little gentle prompting certainly would not go amiss.

The Rooster wants to stay true and loves its family so much that taking chances with relationships is really not up the street of this so cautious individual. But don't be complacent, because even a worm can turn and so it is worthwhile keeping an eye on your Rooster's behaviour.

It is a certain fact that no Rooster could become involved in an affair, or a flirtation, without giving the game away somehow!

1910
1922
1934
1946
1958
1970
1982
1994
2006

The Dog

THE DOG IN LOVE

What a loveable puppy this is, and how easy it is to fall in love with this endearing character. Most Dog people are warm, kind, affable, affectionate and very giving. Of course they are always on the go, so it might sometimes be difficult to keep tabs on them and since they have an extremely healthy imagination, understanding how their minds are working at any point in time may not be all that easy. The Dog can be very indecisive however and hates to make decisions of any sort. This can indicate a character who gets into some terrible scrapes, though without any real intention of causing the sort of chaos that often ensues.

It has been suggested that the Dog, though one of the most likeable individuals, is gifted with loose morals. This is probably to overstate the case since Dog people are quite capable of being faithful and have great integrity, but only if they find themselves living with the right sort of partner. Nevertheless the Dog is inclined to flirtations and even affairs, so that any prospective partner would need to keep his or her eyes wide open.

Dog people love to be loved and would do almost anything to keep a relationship that is important to them. Their imagination is second to none, they are usually intelligent and are always fun to live with. Dog people are very hard workers, but only as long as their interest is present. Dogs love to travel, delight in holidays and are great with children. All in all a good prognosis for success, that is until you fail to keep your eye on the critter for more than five minutes at a time! The decision is yours, but life will never be boring with this character around.

THE FEMALE DOG

This is one of the most endearing characters you are ever likely to meet. However, before you drop the book and dash off to find your female Dog, there are one or two things that you ought to know. For starters, despite her charming nature, winning ways and sexy approach to life, Miss Dog is not the most constant creature in the world and needs plenty of attention if she is to remain locked into the relationship with you. It isn't that she is naturally promiscuous, or that she intends to be unfaithful in any way, and her behaviour is probably a direct result of her lack of basic self-confidence.

This aspect of the Dog throws up an individual whose basic mode of thinking is often at odds with apparent behaviour, which does make the character difficult for some people to come to terms with. The female Dog really needs constant approbation and encouragement if she is to offer the best she can to life - and of course to you. Not that it is difficult to find the time you would require to keep this alliance going, because Miss Dog is such fun to be with.

True, you are going to need plenty of energy and will really only get a rest yourself when she decides to collapse in a heap with sheer exhaustion. Miss Dog can be all things to all men because she has a keen intellect, a sunny disposition, warm eyes and, at times, a red-hot sex drive.

If you still have the desire to proceed, you could hardly choose a more interesting partner, though as in all aspects of life there has to be a price to pay. In this case it might be confusion because believe me, this woman is not always easy to understand. For those who take the chance, the results could be more than worthwhile.

THE MALE DOG

As often turns out to be the case, the male version of this animal does not display itself to the world in quite the same way that his female counterpart would do. There is the same basic lack of self-confidence, though the male Dog is more inclined to cover this with a sense of bravado and is much less likely to rely on you to sort things out once they have gone terribly wrong, which on occasions for the Dog they are almost certain to do.

The male Dog comes across as being very capable, quite dynamic and very keen to get ahead. If you have lived with this person for long however you might already have realised that the truth of the situation is somewhat different.

The male Dog can spend endless hours gazing into the mirror of his own soul, wondering if the decisions he has just taken are right and just, and attempting to weigh up the implications of everything. Indecision is the hallmark of Dog types and as the partner of the Dog, it may often be up to you to do the necessary convincing. All the same, this is an endearing character, who is very easy to love and who will not let you down if he remains happy with his lot in life.

This man is imaginative, intelligent, often good-looking and has a magnetism that he could not disguise, even assuming he wished to do so - which he does not.

Mr Dog can work long and hard, though he probably does not care for getting his hands dirty and would much rather supervise other, less innovative types if he can. He can be especially good at self-employment, but does lack the drive he sometimes desires and sometimes needs a slight shove. A little gentle pressure can achieve a great deal.

THE DOG BEHIND CLOSED DOORS

Light the blue touch paper and stand back, because you are on the receiving end of a real firework here! In reality this might not turn out to be the case, especially if your Dog is tired, lacking in personal esteem or in any way deflated in ego. But when the Dog is firing on all cylinders there is not a better lover to be found anywhere.

Part of the reason why the Dog is in such demand sexually is based on the natural imagination that all Dogs possess. It should also be remembered that these people have the right astrological prerequisites to be experts in the actual mechanisms involved. Put the two together and the recipe looks good - that is as long as you understand that your Dog partner, although proving to be the most forthcoming individual you could imagine, may not actually be with you at all.

This is the fantasy expert of the Chinese zoo and whether male or female, the Dog has a stock of sexual dreams that would fill several large books and still leave some left over. People who really relish the Dog do not worry about this too much, but simply learn to understand that everyone needs to stretch their imagination sometimes, in order to keep things fresh and alive. What might complicate matters a little however is that the Dog is quite capable of jealousy, so that whilst he or she might happily admit to their sexual fantasies, you would probably be better off denying your own. If this seems a little unfair, there is an alternative. Be straight with your Dog partner from the word go. Make a common theme of your thoughts and wishes and play them out together. But let your Dog know that this is all nothing but make-believe.

THE DOG AND CONSTANCY

The Dog is not naturally a wanderer when it comes to relationships, though you might be fooled into believing that this is not the case. There are probably more split relationships amongst Dog people than any other Chinese sign. This is usually due to a breakdown in communication and a failure on the part of the Dog's partner to realise what makes this sign tick. Not that the Dog can be completely absolved from responsibility, but neither can this individual be held responsible for his or her own popularity. The fact is that for any Dog person, there is almost always someone waiting in the wings.

It's true that Dog people are often inclined to have affairs, and is also the case that they would not tolerate such a state of affairs in the case of their own partner. Because of these facts it appears to be difficult to defend the Dog type, yet these are the hardest people in the world to disagree with about anything. At the end of the day people are what they are and a happy Dog would never dream of betraying a relationship under any circumstances.

Keep your Dog feeling warm, protected, intellectually stimulated and sexually satisfied. Deal with these criteria and you have the recipe for what should turn out to be a happy and genuinely fulfilling relationship. If you are taking something of a chance on the way, well, isn't that what life is all about anyway? In these days of failed marriages almost any liaison can go wrong and at least with the Dog you will experience day-to-day happiness of a sort that you may not have dreamed of before. On the way your Dog partner will rain compliments down on you like a tropical monsoon.

1911
1923
1935
1947
1959
1971
1983
1995
2007

The Pig

THE PIG IN LOVE

A complex creature the Pig, and not one that many would find all that easy to understand. Both genders of Pig are deep, sensual, dark and sometimes brooding, yet they are also extremely kind, would do almost anything for anyone and love to nurture. The Pig type is deeply sensitive and yet is likely to stand up to adversity that would have others defeated instantly. Difficulties early on are not unusual in the case of the Pig, so experience comes early and stays with the individual right through life.

Once the Pig gives his or her heart, there is nothing that he or she would refuse to do for the recipient. Perhaps this is part of the reason that the sign is so misused and might also explain why a lack of personal happiness sometimes attends these people. In the cases where this is really obvious Pig types can start to mistrust the whole of humanity and might withdraw from the world of people altogether. Fortunately this is a rarity, because the Pig genuinely does have a great deal to offer.

Pig types are hard workers, tireless parents and ardent lovers. They seldom put themselves first in anything, though can, at the same time, be dreadfully opinionated.

Do you want someone around who would genuinely fight to the death on your behalf if it became necessary to do so? The Pig is just this sort of character. He or she may not be all that good at mouthing the words to say how they feel about you, but they can find ways to prove it, both materially and in more personal ways, and will never tire of showing you their gratitude and affection. No effort on your part would go without notice, even if little or nothing is actually said at the time.

THE FEMALE PIG

Here we have one of the most deeply sensual individuals to be found anywhere. Miss Pig is alluring and carries a sex appeal that would stop a charging elephant in its tracks. You can't usually mistake the female Pig type, because in any room eyes will turn in her direction when she enters. Not that she is usually the most voluble person around, because a few words can go a long way in the case of this individual. Despite this fact many Pig women have a deeply poetical touch and display this as a token of their sensitivity, which runs very deep.

In a love match Miss Pig can be a trifle overpowering for some, less deep types, and you really do have to be the sort of person who wishes to be loved totally in order to stand the pressure that this can imply.

Miss Pig is always helping someone with something and as you become more and more an extension of her own view of life, you will be expected to join in without question. It's very hard to say no to these people, because in their own, quiet way they have tremendous power of a sort that is not generally opposed.

Miss Pig can be as sober as a judge or as mad as a hatter, and you will probably never be able to work out just why this is the case at any particular point in time. She can be deeply insular and then frighteningly flippant.

It's a heady blend and certainly not one that is everyone's cup of tea but if you are the one who is in love with Miss Pig, you are already smitten and would therefore take no notice of contrary advice. So no matter what the world tries to tell you, your own instincts are likely to be the ones that count the most. Don't fight it; love like this is the very rarest sort of all!

THE MALE PIG

Here we have a character who is not always at ease with himself. The very feminine qualities of the Pig do not always sit easily on male shoulders, so unless he is truly a 'new man' some sort of frustrations are likely to show. All the same, Mr Pig is a deeply caring individual and would not let you down in any situation if he could avoid doing so. It's true that he has a long memory and is only really good to those he takes to, but if you are one of them Mr Pig will look after you extremely well.

The male Pig is happy to be at home with his family, and can also make his way in the world. He does have a slightly lazy streak and would be happy to sit around and watch the grass grow from time to time, though this is good for his over-active nervous system.

Once the male porker makes his mind up to do something it is very unlikely that you would be able to change it, and in most situations that you will encounter there is really very little point in trying to do so.

A word of warning might be to look out for a tendency towards a jealous side, which is one of the less endearing qualities of Mr Pig. A good dose of reassurance would probably prevent such a situation, though if Mr Pig does become possessive it is a difficult trait to shift.

When a good meeting of minds is achieved Mr Pig is a good person to know and has the capability to love very deeply. He may be quite literate and even poetical, will have an interest in the mysterious and may also have a special love of places close to water.

Mr Pig is a good and faithful partner most of the time but total trust might be a little difficult here.

THE PIG BEHIND CLOSED DOORS

If it is intensity within a personal relationship that you are looking for, then Mr or Miss Pig should be right up your street. In a sexual sense the Pig is one of the marathon runners of the Chinese zoo and since sensuality at every level is right up this individual's street, sex figures high on the list of priorities. Pigs are not the easiest people to understand however and can be terrible sulkers if things do not turn out the way they would wish. For this reason most individuals would allow a Pig partner to have most of his or her own way, which is not necessarily the right way to proceed.

The Pig may not have the most startling imagination of anyone, or so it could seem at first meeting. The truth is often quite the reverse and all Pigs can 'role play' until the cows come home. If the 'unusual' in love is your thing, then once again you might have chosen wisely with the Pig. However this character would soon tire of conventional love, either in or out of the bedroom, and really does need a partner who is willing and able to ring the changes.

Pigs love to sit up late at night, talking and just generally being together, but as a result could easily still be in bed at lunch time the following day; whilst persuading them to come in out of the sunshine in the summer is almost impossible under any circumstances.

Yes you could be in for a startling love life, but remember, sensuality relates to all the other senses too. Pigs often eat and drink too much and it is virtually impossible to get them out of the bathroom once they are joyfully settled there. The Pig is a sensualist of the most extreme sort, and that could prove to be irritating eventually.

THE PIG AND CONSTANCY

A complex and difficult person to understand, that's the Pig, and whilst most Pigs are definitely into one relationship at a time, this is by no means always the case. The problem here is that life has to be happy right across the board in order to make certain that the Pig is comfortable and settled. We all have our insecurities, but the Pig does have more than most and this might be the chief cause of any real problems that do arise.

Coming to terms with the depth of Pig nature makes it difficult to know what might be troubling your Pig partner, even on those occasions when you know for certain that something is. Pigs can be very different or totally conventional, and all within the space of a few minutes, and you will be expected to keep up with these sudden changes in direction. What is more, if you show too much concern for the Pig you could be accused of being overprotective. Every situation is different, as is each day living with the Pig individual, who meanwhile would explain that they are the simplest person in the world to understand. The fact that they tell you this whilst riding a unicycle and cross-dressing is quite beside the point as far as they are concerned. In the end it is probably best to simply ride the wave of Pig originality, rather than trying to swim against it.

If you want to keep your Pig partner faithful, talk when they want to, remain quiet when they are; be on hand when they are feeling romantic and be a totally dutiful partner. Alternatively, remain your own cheerful self and allow the Pig to see how easy it is to live a life without perpetual intensity and soul-searching. It might do them good!

CHINESE ELEMENTS AND LOVE

In the introductory chapter to this book mention was made of the 60 year cycle that was such an important part of Chinese Astrology, from its earliest roots. This cycle comes about as a result of planetary interaction, but was classified by Ancient Chinese star watchers as 12 periods of 5 years. As a result each animal year also responds to one of five different Elements, which the astrologers of old believed modified the zodiac sign ruling that year. The five elements are Metal, Water, Wood, Fire and Earth.

The Elements follow the animal year signs in turn, so for example, 1960 was the year of the Metal Rat. The Rat also ruled the year 1972 but in this case it was the Water Rat. Not for 60 years beyond 1960 will the world fall under the sway of the Metal Rat once again.

The Elements run independently of the animal signs, yet they do have a great part to play in the way that the signs display themselves. This is especially true in an emotional sense, and there is no greater emotion than love!

For this reason it is important, when assessing the way that any particular person is likely to behave in a specific relationship, not only to know thet animal year in which the individual was born, but also the Element that ruled that year. In the Animal Year list at the start of this book you will also find a list of the Elements, so it's easy to ascertain exactly what animal and Element combination you are dealing with.

Following this page you will find a description of the five Elements and the sort of people they are likely to produce. However life is a little more complicated than this because different Elements affect the 12 signs in a multitude of ways. For this reason I have supplied a reading for every animal and Element combination, which helps you in your search for a more complete understanding of any particular individual.

The bearing that the Elements have on personality and therefore the capacity for love is great, so read on and discover the fact for yourself.

THE CHINESE ELEMENTS

METAL

Metal people tend to be rigid and do not give in easily. They insist on honesty and expect much from a prospective partner. There is great strength of character here, but also a tendency towards dominance.

WATER

Water people are usually thought of as being very creative. There is a compassion and an understanding here that reduces the more caustic qualities of any sign. In love they tend to be yielding and easily influenced.

WOOD

Consideration is the hallmark of Wood types. Warmth, generosity and co-operative attitudes are more evident here and this group of people will always try hard to see the other person's point of view.

FIRE

As the Element itself indicates, Fire makes for a dynamic quality to the nature. In terms of love this brings a sense of honour but can also mean a temperament that is without the flexibility that might be expected.

EARTH

Earth people will wait a long time for love to blossom They can work hard to make others see things their own way, and constantly strive to make relationships work well. This Element can be very stubborn.

THE METAL RAT

Male or female, here we have a character to be reckoned with. All Rats are go-getters and this character much more so than some of his or her elemental cousins. The Metal Rat will have a good chat-up line and will not be lacking in romantic company. However, tying him or her down to anything greater than a flirtation, or more likely an affair, may not be all that easy, because the Metal Rat loves to be independent and to play the field whenever possible.

There is a tremendous sense of urgency here, so the Metal Rat tends to be on the go from morning until night, always has the next 'grand scheme' to deal with, but is capable of significant material success, probably after a few fairly dodgy starts. Some people would say that the Metal Rat is lacking in integrity and in moral scruples, though this might be putting things a little unfairly. There is a magnetic personality present, which makes the character difficult to dislike, and a capacity to live life in the fast lane which might just be a prospective partner's cup of tea.

Whether or not you will ever come to know the Metal Rat as much as you would wish is in some doubt, since we find here an individual whose true character always seems to be changed by prevailing circumstances. The Metal Rat is a good lover, though there may often be something more important at the back of his or her mind and so keeping him or her tied to the same spot can be difficult. Entertainment would always be part of the package, as would a cutting humour, for which this individual is famed. Metal Rat people are often very good-looking and have sex appeal to spare. A real charmer this character, with dynamism to spare.

THE WATER RAT

A quite endearing character this one, since the naturally friendly aspect of the Rat is enhanced by the presence of the Water Element. The Water Rat knows exactly what it wants from life, which is more than could be said for some of its elemental cousins. If one of the wants is you, then you should find yourself being wooed with good old-fashioned courtesy and see a wealth of hearts and flowers entering your life.

The Water Rat is brave and honest (well, as honest as any character born under this sign is capable of being). He or she will certainly set out to sweep you off your feet and having done so, probably finds you in just the position that would suit this quite ardent character best. Crying out for affection him or her self, the Water Rat might possibly be the easiest person in the world to love and generally has so many endearing characteristics that they seem too good to be true.

Here we have a person who is definitely capable of success, though probably not to the same degree as some of the other Rat types. But to compensate, the Water Rat has a charm and charisma that is a delight to know and a sense of the ridiculous that makes for an interesting sort of life. You should never underestimate the Water Rat's intuition, which is strong, or the poetic nature of the individual, which perpetuates longer in this case than with the average Rat.

It would be fair to suggest that the Water Rat does have a healthy temper and that it does not suffer fools gladly, though if you are willing to offer your heart unconditionally, it is very unlikely that you would end up losing anything but your inhibitions. Here we have a person who may be better for knowing.

THE WOOD RAT

It is a fact that the Rat person is one of the most loveable rogues to be found anywhere in Chinese astrology. All Rats are charmers and are quite capable of talking the birds down from the trees. What might sometimes be in doubt is the degree of sincerity that attends their efforts, particularly since, once you turn your back, they could be handing out the same line to someone else. If there is an exception to this rule, it comes in the guise of the Wood Rat, who is more likely to stick to one partner (at least at the same time) and is generally more reliable than most of his of her cousins.

All Rats are generous and this is particularly well marked when the Wood Element is in attendance. Since the Wood Rat is also capable of singular financial success, their generosity might be worth a second look. Not that this character is anyone's fool. The Wood Rat chooses more carefully and does want good value for money, or effort. This means something of a chase to actually tie the Wood Rat down in the first place, but since this is half the fun to such an individual, there should not be many complaints on the way.

Perhaps there is a little less imagination here, but on the other hand there is a more consistent attitude to life, which many potential partners could consider to be a reasonable exchange. But don't let me mislead you. The Wood Rat is exciting, enterprising, always willing to be romantic and has a supply of energy that never seems to be diminished for a moment. If you are the sort to keep up with the character then you could find yourself in for a happy time on the way to exhaustion. Do remember on the way though that you will need some time to yourself.

THE FIRE RAT

The main region of the Fire in this case seems to be in the tail of the Rat, because the speed and agility of this critter is almost beyond belief. This is the natural car salesperson of the Chinese zoo, but one who is prepared to pursue a sale up hill and down dale if it proves to be necessary to do so. If a Fire Rat is looking for a partner, or even a flirtation, and sets its eyes on you, then be prepared for declarations of love beyond the dreams of almost any mortal. Whether or not you actually fall for the line or not depends on whether you are in the market for a new car!

As all grandmothers are apt to advise us, 'Fine words butter no parsnips' and there are plenty of fine words coming from this direction. Not that you should automatically believe that the Fire Rat is shallow.

All Rats can love sincerely and ardently, are usually quite successful in life and invariably get what they want. Mr Fire Rat could be rather jealous by nature, but won't expect you to show the same tendency, whilst Miss Fire Rat turns heads at any social gathering and quite frankly, does need to be watched.

It is always good in life to know what you might be getting, and it is so difficult in the case of Fire Rat to see beyond the torrent of words and the many bunches of flowers, that some careful thinking is called for. The best course of action is a fairly protracted engagement. At least that way you would come to really know your Fire Rat and can make a more considered decision. The worst Fire Rats are not the ones who turn up regularly. These people do not play with your emotions, they mould them like clay!

THE EARTH RAT

It has to be understood that all Rats are go-getters, communicators, and are always on the go. However, if there is any exception to the rule within the Rat family as a whole it may be evident to a degree in the nature of the slightly more steady and careful Earth Rat.

There is certainly an ability to get on in life, which is marked in the case of this individual as it is with all his or her cousins, though the Earth Rat will work longer and harder to achieve a desired objective and might also stay around longer to enjoy the fruits of success once the effort has been put in. As to a deep relationship, well that can only be considered if you actually see the party concerned, and Earth Rats are so busy working diligently that they are often missing from the scene for long periods of time.

Once you do manage to pin them down, which will probably be by the tail, the Earth Rat individual is romantic, full of flowery language, attentive and kind. There is less potential jealousy here than would be the case with the Fire Rat and even a grudging acceptance of your own abilities.

The Earth Rat is capable of being sincere and is less likely than other members of his or her clan to let you down. He or she is a good parent and contributes towards building a happy home. Of course none of this will make sense if you don't know the person concerned, so my advice is not only to live but to work with your Earth Rat. At least by this means you will get to speak to them occasionally and they, in turn, might remember who you are.

All in all a very likeable character however and one who is likely to get better for keeping.

THE METAL OX

The Ox is never going to win any prizes for being the most dynamic person around, though it is possible that the Metal Element would lift the nature a degree or two and bring more vitality to what can be a rather stick-in-the-mud sort of nature.

Don't run away with the idea that the Ox is short on romantic potential. On the contrary, this is one of the most caring of all the Chinese Zodiac signs. Ox people love deeply and often for life. Metal in the nature could mean that they are more likely to express that love in more dynamic ways and that the person concerned would be far more comfortable when it comes to expressing that love in public.

The Metal Ox has a more adaptable nature than most of his or her bovine cousins, though don't be fooled into thinking that this character can be put upon, because nothing could be further from the truth.

The Metal Ox desires a comfortable home, and is more than willing to contribute to making it so. There is great stamina here and this is expressed as readily in personal circumstances as it might be in terms of practical skills, which are also usually present. The Metal Ox will be unlikely to head a rock band, make the next blockbuster movie or buy a top of the range sports car, but he or she will love you day after day, through good or bad. They will usually be there when you need them and show a kindness in adversity which makes most other signs look less than caring by comparison.

If you are considering the Metal Ox as a partner, you are probably quite dynamic yourself. If this is not the case, look again carefully because too many positives in the same house may not work well.

THE WATER OX

There is not a more gentle, or a more caring character to be found than this one. But is that really what you want, hour after hour, day after day? This is a hard act either to follow or sometimes even to live with, mainly because the standards are so very high. The Water Ox invariably gives a part of his or her life to humanity as a whole and can often be found working in a hospital, social services or youth work. However, this is not always the case and the Water Ox does have fairly good executive ability, as long as it is of a structured and steady sort.

Words of affection are sometimes difficult for the Water Ox to express, but do not be fooled. It is certainly not the case that the Water Ox fails to love deeply, merely that he or she finds it rather difficult to communicate the fact. Patience on your part, plus an understanding of the basic nature of the individual will help and might relax the Water Ox to the condition from which they become the most romantic and poetical person you could imagine.

There is a great depth of personality here, if only you can get to the bottom of it, and a love of home and family that is second to none.

This may not be the most entertaining person around. He or she is steady, regular, predictable and a definite follower of routines. But if slow and steady really does win the race, then the Water Ox would get to the line even before the tortoise managed to do so - and may well be carrying a large bag of cash that he or she has managed to amass on the way.

Some would consider this person to be the ideal partner. Maybe you are one of them?

THE WOOD OX

If there is one fact that sets the Wood Ox apart from the rest, it is the ability to get feelings and emotions sorted out successfully and this alone could prove to be crucial in terms of a positive love life. Ox people generally can be very reserved, and that means that explaining their most secret feelings is something they can rarely if ever do. This often leads others to think that the Ox is cool, and nothing could be further from the truth. The slightly less restricted nature of the Wood Ox compensates and proves to be a boon in affairs of the heart.

Not that this is the most driving individual you are ever likely to meet. So much depends on what you are looking for in a partner. Like all Ox people this character is only too willing to work hard and usually gets on well in life practically. Wood Ox people are often in positions of influence and responsibility and so respond well to a settled home life in order to compensate. But the word 'settled' can be translated as 'too comfortable', which might be 'positively tedious' to you.

A little bomb under this individual now and again does no harm, though some subtlety is necessary because nobody could move an Ox simply by shouting the odds or making threats of any kind.

The Wood Ox needs encouragement and coaxing, but he or she also needs excitement, even though the Ox might be the last one to realise the fact.

Physical passion is present here in great measure, and even a degree of good, old-fashioned romance. What might be absent is 'sparkle'. Of course this might be the last thing you are looking for, in which case full steam ahead in your relationship with the steady Wood Ox.

THE FIRE OX

Although the Ox is a plodder by nature, this is not strictly true when Fire is present in the nature. You might have all sorts of problems with the Fire Ox, but finding this person unromantic or apathetic are not likely to figure amongst them. The Fire Ox has strength allied to determination, which is as much a factor in the way this type approaches love as it is in terms of strictly practical matters.

Once the Fire Ox has decided that you are the one, he or she can be very determined in their efforts to win you round. You cannot turn aside from the words of love, the gifts, the attention, and you could easily be flattered into responding. Not that this is necessarily wrong, but once you have committed yourself you actually have to live with the individual concerned, presumably for a long time. At the end of the day an Ox is an Ox is an Ox, and although the Fire version is rather more 'up front' than the rest the bovine characteristics are still present.

If you want stability, financial security, a good potential parent and a caring partner, then look no further. If, on the other hand, you require a riotous night life, excitement seeping out of every pore and unending diversity you might decide to put your hand back into the lucky dip again. No insult is intended here and the Fire Ox has far more attributes than failings. In the right relationship and with the correct encouragement the Fire Ox brings integrity and truth to a world that often lacks both. He or she will always give you good cause to be proud of them, would be unlikely to let you down in any major way and will even demonstrate virtues you may not have been aware of before.

THE EARTH OX

Here we have the Ox to rival them all. Usually last out of bed and first into it the Earth Ox is steady and fastidious. He or she would rarely take any great chances in life and yet probably manages to attract more material success than the rest of the herd put together. A tireless worker and a good planner, the Earth Ox has its sights set on a far distant horizon that you may not even be able to make out, but it is there and the Earth Ox will prove the fact eventually.

You are unlikely to meet the Earth Ox at the disco, the night club or the rock concert, though this individual does tend to be very sporting by nature and is by no means lacking in physical vitality. The Earth Ox type is usually fairly robust in health and is capable of accepting great responsibility without cracking under the strain of it.

Is this person exciting and impulsive? No! Would you find the Earth Ox where you expected them to be, caring and concerned day after day? Yes! But be certain that you know what you are in for. This might not appear to be the lover of the century but when it comes to sex you could be very surprised indeed. The Earth Ox does not lack integrity, always comes good with promises and likes to move onward and upward socially. He or she is probably destined for success of a sort that other signs could never aspire to and there is little that cannot be achieved here, with time and determination.

There is no better parent to be found, or anyone more committed to building up a home that is secure, comfortable and luxurious. Routine rules the roost and tidiness can become something of an obsession, though deep and enduring love is not in doubt.

THE METAL TIGER

It is sometimes suggested that Tiger people are rather detached emotionally and that, like the animal they represent, they are inclined to walk alone. There is an element of truth in this belief but it might turn out to be slightly less true in the case of the Metal Tiger. Metal Tiger people are capable of being cool and even calculating on occasions, but they do have spirit and the ability to bring others round to their point of view.

The Tiger is intellectually aloof on occasions, and in this respect the Metal version of the big cat is no exception. Although Tiger types can mix with almost any type of person, they are inclined to prefer artistic and even abstract types and will support the cause of the starving artist at the drop of a hat. The Metal Tiger is slightly more mainstream in preferences and comes down on the side of originality, rather than peculiarity. Such individuals tend to be good workers and have executive abilities. In relationships their need is for intellectual as well as physical stimulus and they are quite capable of compartmenting their lives. If this sometimes appears to leave you out in the cold, prepare for an aspect of the Metal Tiger that you can either come to terms with or not.

It is very unlikely that this individual would change his or her personality, and certainly not overnight. The fact is that this is not an easy type to understand at all, for he or she often displays a superficiality that lies like a bridge over depths that few could fathom.

Nevertheless the Metal Tiger is a good partner to many, is capable and supportive in a family sense, has few hang-ups and knows how to bring home the bacon.

THE WATER TIGER

Perhaps this is the most difficult member of the Tiger family to understand, mainly because the Tiger person is often cool and even aloof, whilst Water brings greater understanding and a desire to 'nurture' which is probably not all that noticeable in the case of this sign.

Mr or Miss Water Tiger is definitely an interesting person to know and attracts significant attention from others. Such people often work on behalf of the underprivileged, can easily make a niche for his or her self in life and are invariably quite artistic. Being nobody's fool, the Water Tiger does at the same time seem to fall easily for a sob story and is a natural supporter of 'causes'. But the tendency to behave this way can always be justified at an intellectual level and the apparent 'coolness' of the Tiger may still be present.

Rules and regulations mean little to this person and he or she is quite capable of having a good time. Being naturally catholic in tastes the Water Tiger is just as likely to be found at a rock concert or listening to a symphony orchestra. Love to the Water Tiger is much more than cuddles and candy, it is a process of the mind and as such needs to be approached in the same original manner that attends all endeavours. To be on the receiving end can make one feel a little like part of an experiment and this fact would take the fun out of the situation for some.

The Water Tiger really does care about all sorts of things and people. As a lover you will come high on the list, but there is always going to be a list and that is something that you can never get away from. The Water Tiger is paradoxical and very complex.

THE WOOD TIGER

Wood is a useful attribute to the Tiger nature since it is inclined to bring greater warmth and therefore a better understanding on the part of the observer regarding what makes the Tiger individual tick. This breed of Tiger is still a thinker and someone who has a great deal of intellectual stimulus, though there are a greater number of contacts possible with the world at large and also probably a great deal more laughter within the nature.

Wood Tigers are usually good fun to be with, they always know something about every situation and can display their original natures in a number of different ways. Boredom is not likely to attend the life of this character, or those with whom he or she is involved. There is a basic love of life here and a fascination for it that is present with all Tiger people but which in other Elements tends to be internalised. In loving situations the Wood Tiger is gentle and kind, offering a poetic sort of affection that represents true passion to anyone who is really paying attention.

The Tiger's main role in life is to learn, and this is a lifelong process. The Wood Tiger wants to take you along on the journey of discovery and this could mean travel, a variety of different interests and the cultivation of an original and stimulating home base. It is difficult to argue with this individual, mainly because even when they are not behaving fairly, they give the impression that they are. Wood Tigers never get sufficient rest and might run themselves ragged, though a change is as good as a rest and here we have someone who could never, ever be tedious. To many the Wood Tiger represents a real challenge.

THE FIRE TIGER

This is clearly the most positive of all the Tiger family, which means that here we find a person who manages to make a distinct success of his or her life. However, this might not actually be the same as making a promise of conjugal bliss and some care is necessary when approaching a relationship with this individual.

The naturally intellectual bent of the Tiger is added here to the force of the Fire Element, so the Fire Tiger is likely to be fairly dominant by nature and not all that inclined to spend time thinking about what makes you tick. This does not necessarily mean that the Fire Tiger is selfish, merely single-minded.

If you do manage to get this big cat on your side, you could be in for an interesting, stimulating and exciting life, but you will need great energy to cope with the driving pace of everything and could also find that your Tiger partner expects as much of you as of him or her self. If you don't have the stamina necessary, then life could be rather uncomfortable.

The Fire Tiger is a good provider, a constant friend and a supporter of your right to individuality, that is as long as it does not interfere with his or her own plans. You would have to be very clever to better this person in argument but might find the challenge quite stimulating. Fire Tigers do a great deal for the world and can be massive idealists. The problem is that they are so committed to projects outside the home that you may rarely see them at all. When they are around they will love you with a passion and are not likely to wander far from you emotionally. A hard act to match but there is never a dull moment here.

THE EARTH TIGER

If there is one sign of the Chinese Zodiac that really does need to be brought down to earth, it surely has to be the Tiger and it is likely that the combination of the Element, together with the natural Tiger nature, makes a very potent and useful fusion.

The Earth Tiger has all the thoughts, the incentive, the questioning mind and the thirst for life of all the breed but he or she is steady, controlled and more likely to spend time nurturing relationships. This is an individual who would never prove tedious to have around and who would always have something interesting to say. The capacity for love that is held in this breast can surprise almost anyone and is the basis of great happiness within a romantic attachment - as long as certain facts are understood.

The Earth Tiger does not like to be tied down, but is quite likely to perform the exercise for itself. There is a psychologically motivated desire for security and contentment here, but it comes through at an instinctive level and needs to be left to the Tiger to recognise. A fairly long and not too intense build-up to the relationship would probably work best, leaving the Earth Tiger to set the different stages. Any feeling that pressure is being put upon it may send the Earth Tiger running for the jungle and it is worth remembering that slow and steady definitely does win the race here.

This is never going to be an individual who responds to routines and as long as the changes are rung on a regular basis there may be the seeds here of a relationship bloom that would flower for many a happy year. Much of the effort needed is merely a case of being one step ahead of the varying needs of this fascinating type.

THE METAL RABBIT

The Rabbit is a lovely person, on this fact most people would agree. Of course this is not the same as suggesting that this is someone who is always easy to understand, or to deal with in a deeply personal sense. Things may be slightly less complicated in the case of the Metal Rabbit however because this animal type is better at coming to terms with its own peculiarities and at dealing with them.

The Rabbit is kind, warm, sincere and very loving. Most Rabbits settle for a happy home life and a stable relationship, which is certainly true of the Metal bunny. Being a natural when it comes to understanding others, the Metal Rabbit will sort out all your own hang-ups and will always be on hand to lend the sort of support that other signs would never even think of. The Metal Rabbit also has the capacity to combine a fairly stable emotional nature with the ability to succeed in a material sense, which should mean a Rabbit partner with a decent earning capacity.

All Rabbit types are good lovers, but their natures do run deep and they need to feel very secure. The emotional fur of the creature needs constant brushing and the Metal Rabbit is certainly no exception in this regard. This is probably the only aspect of life with the Metal Rabbit that needs absolute attention, because once this person is firmly on the tracks of life, there is no deviation. Since the Metal Rabbit was born to look out for the virtues of wedded bliss, much of the running is his or hers to make and you should never go short of either attention or kind words. The Metal Rabbit is a bottomless pit and you can pour your own love into it from now until eternity without any hope of reaching the rim.

THE WATER RABBIT

Although this is, without doubt, the most likeable and friendly of all the Rabbit clan, it is not necessarily the easiest to understand. The emotional nature of all Rabbits runs deep, but never more so than in the case of the Water Rabbit, who is practically unfathomable. For this reason you don't always know where you stand with him or her and you could find it hard to come to terms with a nature that you fail to comprehend.

On a practical, day-to-day level, the Water Rabbit is kind and loving, adores his or her family and wants to enjoy a happy and settled sort of home life. The Water Rabbit is a good worker, usually in some capacity that involves being of use to society as a whole. Water Rabbit people love animals, sometimes even more than they care for people, and yet the humanitarian tendencies of this character are always obvious.

As a lover the Water Rabbit is second to none, being gentle and attentive, demonstrative and imaginative too. It has been suggested that the physical side of love is where the Water Rabbit is at its best, a fact that is aided by the Rabbit's natural affinity with the sensual in life, especially at a sexual level.

Constancy could be something of a problem here, and particularly so if the the Water Rabbit is unhappy in any way. This Chinese sign is probably more inclined to wander in any case, and with the Water Element also present, the tendency is even greater. With love and understanding comes happiness however, and this is the surest recipe for a prolonged and happy union. The Water Rabbit should ensure that life does not become too complicated or too routine. Both are equally destructive to this character.

THE WOOD RABBIT

Is the Wood Rabbit really cut out for the sort of life that means dedication to a particular relationship? The answer to this question is about as elusive as the gates of the Celestial City and depends almost entirely on the sort of partner that the Wood Rabbit chooses in the first place. There is love here of the total sort, but it is also of a unique kind that needs to be fully understood.

The Wood Rabbit cares very much for others. Many of the world's missionaries, charity workers and social philanthropists have been born as Wood Rabbits. There is total commitment and absolute dedication on offer here, and it is of a very practical kind. This side of the Wood Rabbit is almost certain to show in all cases and it might be the seeds of some disappointment if it is not utilised sensibly. So much does this individual give to the person next door, the woman down the road, friends, relations, charitable causes and heaven knows what else, that there isn't always a great deal left for you. Of course, if you actively want to live with a saint, then fine, but most people really would rather not.

But none of this should blind the reader to the fact that this level of giving is quite genuine. There is no thought of personal gain attached and the Wood Rabbit does what it does, simply because it must. Perhaps the best way to deal with the situation is to pitch in and be part of the scenario. At least this way you will see plenty of your Wood Rabbit and then he or she is certain to remember who you are.

The Wood Rabbit can be a paragon, though there are those who will assert that any kind of Rabbit is capable of being a pest - even saintly ones!

THE FIRE RABBIT

All Rabbits follow the same basic pattern, so you should not expect the Fire Rabbit to be all that different from its cousins in the warren, and yet in some ways there are subtle distinctions that could mean a great deal in a personal relationship.

For starters the Fire Rabbit does have at least one paw in reality. Rabbits are often accused of being over-idealistic and of viewing a world as they would wish it to be, not as it really is. This is very much less emphasised in the case of the Fire Rabbit, who although every bit as kind and helpful as all the bunny breed, is also a realist. This almost certainly means a greater degree of personal success and also tends towards a more realistic view of relationships.

Your Fire Rabbit is fond of his or her burrow and is especially geared towards family matters. The Fire Rabbit is an excellent lover, or at the very least tends to suit most other types, thanks to its flexibility and general love of sex. He or she is likely to be very supportive and will always allow you to maintain your own point of view, though might show a very slight jealous streak on occasions. Rest and relaxation are essential and this is where you can make your own influence show.

All Fire Rabbit people have a good interest in life at all its levels and are inclined to adapt to suit your likes and dislikes too. Such a partner will be first and foremost a good friend however and does not really want to settle for a parallel and independent sort of relationship. The Fire Rabbit can be very wise, is invariably fairly psychic and usually knows how any given situation is likely to turn out eventually.

THE EARTH RABBIT

This character is probably the kindest and most sensitive Rabbit of the whole family and is also certainly the easiest to get on with. There are very few people born under this combination who could be considered to be in any way backbiting, callous or selfish. Even these facts could cause a certain degree of difficulty however because the Earth Rabbit is difficult to match in terms of nature and can be a frustrating person to have around as a result.

With regard to personal partnerships, the Wood Rabbit expects a great deal of itself and makes self-approbation into an art form. There is nothing more infuriating to many people than having someone constantly being willing to sacrifice their own desires in life on the altar of selflessness. In fact most of us would find this to be a problem, if only because it makes us feel a little guilty about our own behaviour. As a result the Wood Rabbit, though a truly 'nice' person, could drive you up the wall, and the more so because they are certain to apologise for doing so.

If all or any of this sounds a little negative, do be assured that here we have no 'holier than thou' sort of person. On the contrary, the Earth Rabbit may appear perfect to you, but it does not always like itself too much. Your Earth Rabbit will be helpful, extremely loving and usually quite practical. Family concerns invariably come first and in any case the whole world is simply an extended family to this person. Behind closed doors many people would tell you that the Earth Rabbit is a lover who turns out to be second to none. With imagination, charm, warmth and a smile as wide as a house how could you fail to fall in love with the Earth Rabbit?

THE METAL DRAGON

An interesting individual this, if you can actually get close enough to know him or her. Dynamic, driving, always in command and probably formidable, the Metal Dragon has enough energy to serve an army and a desire to succeed in life that puts this type out on its own. Almost everything is a competition to this character, so that even a simple game of tennis could seem like the All England Finals. Intellectually the Metal Dragon can be quite aloof, and this is part of the reason why this individual is not all that approachable. Invariably the Metal Dragon is clever. This is not the problem, which stems much more from the fact that the Metal Dragon recognises its own cleverness and may elevate it into genius. Whether or not you concur with this belief remains to be seen, but the Metal Dragon does not like to be disagreed with and is usually surrounded by less dominant types in any case.

The Metal Dragon can make a good lover, that is if he or she ever gains humility. All the material aspects of life are quite easily taken care of, and were it only money that you were after, this would be an admirable candidate. On the positive side however there is a great nobility here and an honesty that can be quite disarming. The Metal Dragon is not likely to let you down deliberately and usually sticks to one partner, as long as things are going well. You can expect an opposite who is a good talker, and someone who carries through all intentions to the ultimate conclusion. This sign and Element is not everyone's choice, and the success of such a relationship is mainly dependent on the nature and desires of the prospective partner. The Metal Dragon needs to be loved - but might sometimes expect to be obeyed too.

THE WATER DRAGON

If you think it is likely that the Water Element here would put out the natural flames that eminate from all Dragons, then you could be in for something of a shock, because all members of this species are capable of scorching anyone and everyone from time to time. All the same, this is probably a much easier character to get along with than certain other members of the clan, if only because Water bestows a certain degree of tact, which makes it easier to put up with other traits that are endemic to the Dragon.

It isn't that a Water Dragon partner is always right about everything, it's merely that they have the ability to convince you that they are. Only later, and possibly at a distance, will you realise that you have probably been duped, and by the time you do, chances are that it will be too late to do anything about the situation. But the Water Dragon is kind, sociable and brave. He or she will be unlikely to let you down and if ever the adage 'My word is my bond' could be said to be true, it certainly is in this case.

Routines are definitely out with this character around and you should find life to be both interesting and extremely varied. The Water Dragon is a hard worker, makes light of adversity and cherishes its family.

In a personal sense the Water Dragon may turn out to be deeper and more emotional than would at first seem to be the case. There is a sensitivity here that may not show to the world at large but which is obvious to someone who has greater experience of the nature concerned. This is quite a handful but by no means a person lacking in charm, intelligence or personal success.

THE WOOD DRAGON

Although the Dragon is sometimes seen as being a little 'cold' this is not really the truth at all. The fact is shown more clearly in the case of the Wood Dragon than would seem to be possible in the case of any of its scaly cousins. The Wood Dragon is luckier than the rest because it is better able to demonstrate its love, compassion, bravery and honesty. This makes for a person who is easier to get to know in the first place and who is more understandable to the rest of humanity.

Don't be misled however. The Wood Dragon is just as direct, every bit as determined and quite as definite as any other sort of Dragon. Materially you can expect both the male and female type to exhibit significant success. Much of this will be reflected in your own life if you form a relationship with such a type and the only sacrifice you will have to make is to go along with the thinking of this most original character.

The Wood Dragon is a deep and passionate lover, has much to offer in a family sense, but is always busy and so therefore may not be at home as much as other Chinese sign individuals would. He or she is also a clear individual and does not 'merge' into relationships so much as take part in them.

This is certainly a caring Dragon and is not afraid to speak words of love or to demonstrate its affection in very tangible ways.

As the basis for a relationship a demanding partner would not suit the Wood Dragon, who although considerate of others is still bound to be an individual. Expressing this desire for personal space is part of what the Wood Dragon is about, so that he or she would not willingly relinquish it, no matter what the alternative might be.

THE FIRE DRAGON

Are you a dynamic and fairly dominant sort of person yourself? If the answer to this is 'yes' than the plain and simple advice is to leave the Fire Dragon lurking in its cave. This is probably the most explosive combination of sign and Element to be found anywhere in the Chinese zoo and there is little doubt that the Fire Dragon is at his or her best with a partner who is willing to follow rather than to lead.

No situation is one-sided however and the Fire dragon is a person of great ideals. You always know where you are with this individual, even if the 'where' is half way up a mountain or skiing down a giant glacier. Of course the Fire Dragon will be more than willing to take you along, and will expect you to be just as intrepid as he or she is. Most people who partner this sign are just as happy to stay at home and wait for the return of the prodigal, if only because one risk-taker in a family is probably enough.

The Fire Dragon is always busy, invariably successful and inevitably opinionated. In argument few would match up to the flow of words that come naturally from this direction and it is probably better not to try. Passive resistance might be the answer, though if you know your Fire Dragon well, you will develop your own way of dealing with the flames and smoke that sometimes attend this individual.

The Fire Dragon is always enthusiastic and usually takes relationships very seriously. This is not the most humorous person you will ever meet, though you might be able to do without too many jokes in exchange for the material success that is also usually present. This is a unique character, with no duplicity or pretentions.

THE EARTH DRAGON

This is not a Dragon who moves with lightning speed, though such terms are relative because the Earth Dragon would seem to be no slouch when compared with other Chinese signs. All the same the Earth Dragon is more considered than many of its counterparts and is also willing to stop and think about things, which other Dragon types simply refuse to do. To many this would point towards a greater potential success within a personal relationship, if only because the ability to see the other person's point of view is very important in any coming together.

The Earth Dragon tends to be kind, and will often support an underdog. This Element is not quite so competitive as some of the others, though it should be remembered that all Dragon types have a spirit that makes it difficult for them to stay away from any form of contest. Mr or Miss Earth Dragon is a lover of home and will strive to create a warm and congenial atmosphere for all concerned. Friendship is important to this type of Dragon, and this applies within a deep attachment too, for although the Earth Dragon needs passion and is an undoubted expert in the bedroom, he or she also needs the sort of stability that is not sexually based.

The Earth Dragon is inclined to look before it leaps, but it does leap and the fact that the individual is not shouting the odds all the time should not lead the observer to believe that there is no fire or spirit present. On the contrary, because there is a degree of considered action here, the Earth Dragon would make a formidable opponent and is quite prepared for a long and drawn out struggle if necessary. To many this would seem to be the most approachable Dragon of them all!

THE METAL SNAKE

The Snake is a careful character, not at all inclined to take unnecessary risks and always aware of the direction he or she is taking in life. On some occasions this could make for a less than dynamic sort of individual, though the situation is slightly different in the case of the Metal Snake.

The Snake person is passionate, and never more so than in the case of this member of the clan. You would be unlikely to go short of the sort of attention that makes you feel both loved and protected and can rely on your Metal Snake to find the right words of love to fit any given circumstance.

The Metal Snake is kind, sympathetic and willing to do anything necessary to show its concern for the world at large and for you in particular. The Metal Snake also shows a distinctly practical side and is a good worker and provider. The depth of sensitivity might sometimes be a problem however, since this can be a stumbling block when it comes to absolute progress in life.

If you have a slightly harder edge, this could spell a successful partnership, for the Metal Snake is certainly willing to listen to your point of view.

A word of warning. The Metal Snake will not be pushed into anything, though if you approach him or her in the right way, you should be able to get exactly what you want by other means. All Metal Snakes make really good friends, but awful enemies, because although they are basically kind, they can sometimes bear a grudge. Your Metal Snake knows how to look after you, but might not be quite so good at looking after him or her self. Part of this task will be down to you and won't always be easy.

THE WATER SNAKE

Most real snakes turn out to be good swimmers, which basically means that they are at home in the water element. The same is true of Water Snake people, for the sign and the Element tend to make for a generally positive combination, even if it is sometimes one that is a little quieter than average. What you find first here is great depth and the sort of sympathy which shows this individual on a personal crusade to sort out the world as a whole. The Water Snake does not take at all kindly to rules and regulations and does not care for being told how to behave. All the same, this character would do almost anything for anyone. This is no paradox because the situation is entirely down to motivation.

Trying to force a Snake down any path it did not care for would be the same as pushing a piece of rope. Avoid doing so and use a combination of intuition and flattery, which is almost certain to work. Make certain that your Water Snake gets plenty of variety in life because this person can work for months on end without a break, even though this is the last thing that he or she should really do.

Water Snakes are deeply sensual. They love to eat, to bathe, and most of all they revel in a happy and imaginative sex life. Variety is the spice of life to this individual, even if he or she does not necessarily realise the fact. A contented Water Snake will always stay around and since this is the easiest person in the world to please, you should enjoy the congenial company for a long time.

The Water Snake can be a wonderful companion, a true friend and an excellent lover, so that the effort you have to put in is invariably worthwhile.

THE WOOD SNAKE

Although the word 'lazy' may not directly apply to Snake people, it is sometimes difficult to get them motivated. The Wood Snake may well be the exception here because this is a person who will think about any given situation long and hard before pushing ahead in a planned direction, usually achieving the desired goal with comparative ease. However, this does make the Wood Snake rather single-minded, which itself could be seen as a less than positive trait to some. Once in full flow, the Wood Snake can only see the horizon before it and that might mean that there will be occasions when you take second place.

Like all Snake types, the Wood variety is a sensualist at heart and is happiest when eating, drinking, sleeping or making love. Wood Snakes like to relax out of doors and have a great desire to take their clothes off to make the most of any pleasant weather that is about. As a result this is the sunbather of the Snake fraternity, so that holidays are usually spent near the beach.

As a lover the Wood Snake is good to have around and is a person who shows a great sense of responsibility - at least when he or she is not sleeping. The Wood Snake is tidy and will not clutter the bedroom floor with clothes - but will probably not be very happy about you doing so either. There are some demands from the relationship and it would be fair to say that not everyone would get on equally well with a type that can be a little pedantic on occasions.

All the same, there is little to find fault with here and plenty to set the Wood Snake apart as being what many might consider to be a particularly good catch.

THE FIRE SNAKE

The snake is generally happy to be left alone and is not a creature who would want to provoke unnecessary trouble. The same is generally true of Snake people. But animal and person alike, if cornered, the Snake can make a formidable enemy. This is certainly true in the case of the Fire Snake, who is always ready to strike if it proves to be necessary. You often get the impression with this individual that you are looking at a primed bomb and it is definitely best not to light the fuse if you can avoid doing so.

Fire Snakes have a long memory, but they are loyal, honest, hard-working and very kind to those they take to. In personal relationships they can usually be relied upon to remain faithful to the bitter end and will work long and hard to achieve their desired objectives in life. Although the Fire Snake may not prove to be quite so verbally romantic as some of its reptile cousins, we do have a person here who understands the meaning of the word 'passion', and who is able to lift relationships to previously unsuspected heights on occasions.

Your Fire Snake loves luxury but is willing to forego almost anything in the interests of love if it proves to be necessary to do so. The motivations of the person are sometimes quite hard to understand but there is a basic continuity which at least makes the Fire Snake reliable and, to a certain extent, predictable.

The Fire Snake is happiest in a relationship with a partner who is able to make some of the running and who is willing to step up the excitement, which if left to the Fire Snake, might sometimes be missing. Not an easy person, but someone with integrity and great charm.

THE EARTH SNAKE

The Snake is not the most go-ahead character to be found and the Earth Snake is certainly the least dynamic of the family. This is not to suggest that Mr or Miss Earth Snake is without interest however because male or female, this is a fascinating person, with plenty to offer life and a great deal to contribute to relationships. Not that this shows at first meeting though, and you will need to take a little time out to get to know the person concerned before you formulate any opinion.

The Earth Snake loves to be loved and puts plenty of effort into relationships of all sorts. He or she is probably the most family minded of all the Snakes and is also possibly the best homemaker. Being by nature reserved, this does not mean to say that your Earth Snake is necessarily quiet, especially at home.

Earth Snakes have their own personal zest for life and can do much to infect you with a sort of quiet enthusiasm that is almost totally compulsive. The Earth Snake can generally be trusted, has plenty of power to build a solid career, but can appear to be terribly lazy on occasions.

Here we have an individual who needs desperately to be needed and who can visibly wilt if put into circumstances that do not appeal to the depth of emotion available. The Earth Snake is often happy to take a back seat, or at the very least to co-operate and is unlikely to be a 'go-getter' in the strict sense of the word.

Most people report that the Earth Snake is a fantastic lover, being full of ingenuity and imagination when it comes to a romantic encounter. Beware of the Earth Snake who is a professional sensualist however.

THE METAL HORSE

Arriving at the stables we now find ourselves confronted with the most positive and yet probably the most elusive member of the Horse clan. In a way this is a paradox because, being Metal ruled invariably inclines to greater self-discipline, something which the Horse generally is rather short of. But the reason the Metal Horse is elusive is precisely because he or she always has something else to do. However, once tied down, the Metal Horse is also potentially the most successful member of the herd.

The Metal Horse is intuitive, quick-thinking, resourceful, charming and talented. He or she may also be capricious, vague, unpredictable and unreliable. So much depends on the situation and on the nature of the relationship that it is impossible to be specific about such an original type of person. To many people the Metal Horse is everything that they could possibly want. If you are such an individual, then you are making what clearly must be the right choice. All the same, you are not likely to be in for the steadiest sort of life and should be prepared to be amongst the first out of bed and the last into it. The Metal Horse can dance all night, work all day and then show a great desire to go out dancing once again.

Full of ingenuity, the Metal Horse is always looking for the next port of call and is certainly not the most potentially faithful person you will ever meet. Infidelity is not inevitable though, and especially not if your Metal Horse is living the sort of varied life that he or she relishes most. And although you might find this match confusing, tiring and sometimes infuriating, life will never be dull and there will always be something to look forward to.

THE WATER HORSE

If you want someone in your life who can sort out all your troubles at a stroke and who can make you feel like the most important person who has ever lived, you are almost certain to take to the Water Horse instantly. On the other hand, it may be the selfsame character who has given you so much to worry about in the first place, so that, at the end of the day, you are left with the endless compliments. But don't get confused about this, the Water Horse means everything that he or she says - at the time they say it. This person is not untruthful - simply forgetful. At least the Water Horse is truly concerned with your welfare, as all Horse types are, and this character has the ability to reach deep down into your soul.

The Water Horse is often a natural poet and looks at life through eyes of such wonder that it is difficult not to find yourself travelling on the same fairground ride yourself. This may be no bad thing and at least the Water Horse can send you soaring high above the routine cares of life, though your landing could be a different story and depends entirely on how much notice you take of the rhetoric.

The Water Horse has every intention of being faithful and in fact is full of good intentions of every sort. But as all our grandmothers were apt to say: 'The path to hell is paved with good intentions', so it is just as well to be aware of the bad as well as the good points of this charmer.

You would not find a more likeable person if you were to travel the length and breadth of the four winds. And this is where you will have to go if you ever want to know what makes your Water Horse tick. Most people decide in the end simply to accept what they find.

THE WOOD HORSE

The Chinese Horse person is often accused of being intellectually superior. In the main this accusation is grossly unfair, because the Horse individual is truly egalitarian and does not differentiate between types. If there is a problem here it stems from the fact that the Horse person is usually rather intelligent and expects everyone to share his or her rather unusual interests. The situation is rather different in the case of the Wood Horse however, who finds it much easier to realise that there may be a different point of view and that not all thought processes work exactly the same.

This is not to suggest that the Wood nag is any easier to tie down than any of his or her cousins in the herd, but it does make for a more comfortable point of reference under most circumstances and can lead to a more secure relationship scenario. You may still be infuriated by the Wood Horse's inability to stay in the same place for very long and by its capacity for activity, which seems to be perpetual. You will need both energy and concentration if you want to keep up, whilst if you choose not to do so, you could get the impression that you are being left behind.

The Wood Horse is a great charmer, who can always find just the right words of love to deflate any potentially difficult situation, but he or she is also a very good talker, so expecting to win an argument when one does come along might be a mistake on your part.

It is best to have your case set in steel and not to back down to the constant string of excuses, well-argued rhetoric and plain distractions that flow like honey from the mouth of this most eloquent individual.

THE FIRE HORSE

By far and away the most dynamic member of the herd, the Fire Horse is one of the most entertaining people you would ever want to meet, is impressive and noble and often very good-looking. The Fire Horse is a natural leader and a good fighter - though only in a verbal sense. To beat this character in argument is virtually impossible and so it is best not to try. Not that arguments will occur all that often, as long as the Fire Horse is left alone to deal with its own life in its own way. Difficulties are only really likely if the Fire Horse is constantly thwarted or perpetually told that its point of view is not the correct one for all concerned.

Here we have an individual who is difficult to understand, but who may not be quite as deep as they like to give the impression of being. A fairly casual approach to relationships should not be allowed to mask the fact that the Fire Horse is often really trying to make things work out well.

There is tremendous kindness here and the need for a personal relationship to be based on friendship as much as passion, even though the Fire Horse also has the capacity to be a wonderful lover.

Holding tight to the Fire Horse is impossible, though if you allow this type to do more or less what they wish, making it obvious that you also intend to carry on in your own sweet way, they may never wander far from you at all.

Underlying the confident exterior is a small child who really does not know how to behave properly in love situations and who is not half so self-assured as might at first seem to be the case.

A complex person - but great fun to be with.

THE EARTH HORSE

This is without a doubt the most steady member of the Horse family and one that is incredibly easy to get along with. The reason seems to be that the Earth Horse is more quiet, considered and sensible than the rest of the herd and so is more willing to listen to what you have to say. This is not to suggest that you would find this character to be quiet by inclination, since no Horse is. All the same, you will find that there are slight lulls in the conversation during which you can insert your own opinions and expect them to be at least considered.

The Earth Horse will always be willing to help you with your career and is of tremendous support in a personal sense too.

Here we have a person who knows what he or she wants and who will go to almost any lengths to get it, except, that is, for upsetting you. Insecurity is bound to be present, as it is with all people born under the sign, but the Earth Horse is more likely to recognise its presence and to deal with it sensibly.

In a deeply personal sense the Earth Horse is more inclined than its cousins to stay at home from time to time and is likely to get more rest than the others.

Still wild and free at heart, the Earth Horse is good to be with and can provide a wealth of entertainment, even when times are difficult. You are unlikely to go short of attention or affection and should find this type of Horse to be a more than adequate lover in most senses of the word.

This is a noble and aspiring individual and is usually more constant than the group as a whole. Some people would suggest that here we have the ideal Horse type.

THE METAL GOAT

Although usually cheerful and easy to get on with, the Goat tends to be a fairly quiet sort of person at heart. This is probably less true in the case of Metal Goat, who is more likely to be the life and soul of the party from time to time. But he or she is still a home-bird at heart and is unlikely to want to be on the go from morning until night. The Metal Goat is a shrewd operator in business and can usually be considered as successful. Metal Goats are creative and always want bright, sunny homes with plenty to look at but also with room to move and breathe.

Relationships are very important to Goat types and especially to the Metal Goat, who sees home, family and lover as the motivating factors when it comes to the more practical aspects of life. Goats are kind-hearted and with this character around you won't have to look very far for hearts and flowers, which usually abound in a relationship such as that created by the Metal Goat.

Outside of home the Metal Goat loves to travel, but would probably rather do so in your company and would always yearn for the security of home surroundings when away for protracted periods.

The Metal Goat is open-minded, free and liberal thinking. This is not a person who would generally walk out on any relationship that stood any chance of working, and the Metal Goat deals philosophically with the ups and downs that are a natural part of any personal attachment. However it should be remembered that the Metal Goat will only take so much and once a decision has been made, this is not the sort of person who would go back on his or her word.

THE WATER GOAT

The hardest part of any relationship that involves the Water Goat will probably be getting to know the person in the first place. This is a Goat of high and secret places, a wistful creature who is difficult to track and pin down. The Water Goat is usually at ease with his or her self and sometimes refuses to step out of the shadows to take the chance with anyone else in a deep relationship. Once you do manage to tie the Water Goat down however, you should find that you are living with a truly remarkable person and one who it will take you a lifetime to fully understand.

Many astrologers would say that Water, as an Element, suits the Goat better than any other. Certainly this is a person who is invariably 'in tune' both with self and with life as a whole. Often deeply spiritual by inclination, the Water Goat wants to know much more about the world than can be taken in with a cursory glance. This individual, though usually successful, is rarely a materialist and sets much more store by happiness of spirit than the weight of a purse. As a result the Water Goat's home will probably be simple and cheerful and is invariably suffused with love.

There are drawbacks to any nature though. In the case of the Water Goat there is sometimes an avoidance of responsibility and too much reliance on others. Really important aspects of life are often ignored and decisions too long delayed. All the same it would be difficult to hold anything against the Water Goat for very long and in any case this is an individual who is more likely to form a relationship with someone who is naturally more assertive and who has a better feel for the material in life.

WOOD GOAT

Here we find a very sensitive Goat indeed and there is always going to be a need to bear the fact in mind in your dealings with the Wood version of this animal sign. Although kind, giving, warm and quite sociable, the Wood Goat is capable of withdrawing inwardly to such a distance that it becomes almost impossible to reach. Problems thus caused may well be avoided altogether if you, as the partner of the Wood Goat, keep a check on matters at an earlier stage.

The Wood Goat is a natural home-bird, can sometimes come across as being distinctly timid and yet, when the chips are down, is probably as tough as old boots. This is the sort of apparent paradox which is often thrown up by astrology and is especially noticeable when Wood and the Goat come together. It isn't really when this individual is under pressure that problems are likely to arise but rather when there is too much time to think about things, which is why the Wood Goat is better in a busy and entertaining environment. It is more or less up to you to supply this because if you are a more dominant type you will be called upon to take the lead.

None of this is to suggest that the Wood Goat fails to be practical, creative and even inspirational on occasions, for this is the person who would make the best colleague to have on a desert island.

The Wood Goat is resourceful, and capable of feeding the whole family for almost nothing. In many respects this relationship is going to be a challenge but the chances are that it will be an enjoyable one.

The Wood Goat is very amorous and always wants to please you. What more could you realistically ask of anyone?

THE FIRE GOAT

Now here is an interesting combination, and one that could just surprise you at almost every turn. The reason is that the Goat person is invariably fairly quiet, reserved and sometimes difficult to get to know. Add to this the passion and drive that comes from the Fire Element and a fascinating series of possibilities becomes apparent. The Fire Goat often smoulders for long periods of time before suddenly bursting into emotional flames that can be a terrible shock to the observer. It takes a keen eye and real understanding to see what is happening in advance and so you really have to be on the ball.

As to the general nature of the Fire Goat there is little on the surface to distinguish it from that of almost any member of the Goat family. The Fire Goat is warm and loving, affectionate and generous of spirit. Capable and competent in almost anything that takes his or her fancy the Fire Goat can sail the seas of life without seeming to cause much in the way of a ripple - but not always.

It tends to be in the depths of personal relationships that the true nature of this rather complicated type is really seen. The Fire Goat has passion beyond belief and is reputed to be one of the best lovers in the whole Chinese zoo. When in love the Fire Goat becomes more voluble, has tremendous sex appeal and will do almost anything to secure the relationship that is most desired. There is a power here that flashes like lightning and which could take the most dominant individual by surprise. Simply because it is so unexpected it can be either wonderful or devastating.

You may see the most excessive traits of this individual once a year or barely once in a lifetime.

THE EARTH GOAT

Probably a combination that shows its best traits through the female rather than the male variety, the Earth Goat is friend to almost everyone and a parent to the world. The 'Earth Mother' sort of individual is best typified by this combination and the result is a steady and secure nature, with less of the inherent emotional problems that seem to beset some of the other players in the Goat ensemble. The Earth Goat has persistence and perseverance, will always help you out of a crisis and is loyal to the bitter end.

There is a great 'make do and mend' mentality and, a little like the Fire Goat, the Earth variety is capable of making a delicious 'something' from an apparent 'nothing'. Sewing machine, woodworking tools, plumbing kit - all these are grist to the mill of the Earth Goat, who could make a silk purse out of a sow's ear in no time at all. Male or female alike, your clothes will be washed and socks darned - and sometimes you might be darned infuriated by the whole procedure. It is possible for someone to be too capable and caring, and the Earth Goat proves the point.

Yet there are a multitude of virtues here for the taking and a warmth and depth of spirit that few other sign types could equal. Being earthy, this person is also something of a sensualist, delighting in good food, good drink, sensory stimuli of all types and is especially fond of a good, active sex life. Of course it all really depends on what it is you are looking for. If you want a house in the forest, filled with homespun furniture and a knitted car which runs on fresh air - the Earth Goat might well be for you. Just don't turn into an organic vegetable yoursef as a result!

THE METAL MONKEY

The Monkey is hardly a shy creature, well not in Chinese astrological terms at least. On the contrary, all Monkeys are fairly ego-centred and very sure of themselves. Nowhere is this more true than in the case of the Metal Monkey.

Here we have a character who is a natural leader, a resourceful and capable worker and an admirable lover. Part of the reason lies in the fact that whilst some signs and Elements promise much and deliver little, the Metal Monkey is quite prepared to see any situation through to its most successful conclusion. The Metal Monkey is capable of taking on a demanding job, a complicated home life and a deep attachment, keeping each situation separate and yet dealing with them all in a competent manner.

The Metal Monkey can be a terrible brag and really does have to be at the head of everything. Being the boss in this household would probably mean a constant struggle and though the Metal Monkey truly wants to be egalitarian, it is not likely that he or she will achieve such lofty ideals. All the same, as long as you are willing to pretend that you are toeing the line, all should be well. Routine and sameness bore this character rigid, so you can expect a flexible and ever changing routine, with plenty of social stimulus and an interesting sex life.

It stands to reason that the Metal Monkey is a hard worker and that means that the deeper qualities of home life may sometimes have to give way to more practical successes. This does not prevent the Metal Monkey from being a good parent and a generally faithful partner. But can you put up with someone who expects to get their own way so very much?

THE WATER MONKEY

If some members of the Monkey family are accused from time to time of not being entirely rational, then this is a taunt which is less likely to be levelled at the Water Monkey. The Monkey is essentially a fiery sort of creature and so a little Water in the nature tends to quell some of the flames, making for a warmth that does not consume anything and everything in the vicinity.

The first thing you may notice about the Water Monkey is what a very pleasant person you are dealing with. Of course you should not be fooled. Whilst superficially the Water Monkey gives every impression of joining forces with the human family as a whole, he or she is really out there to gain what they can from any given situation. Not that this really represents either duplicity or deception, it simply is the kind of person that a Water Monkey is. Relationship-wise this can make for an individual who is a little difficult to understand, but one who is nonetheless friendly and approachable. The Water Monkey is capable of loving with a passion and is especially fond of a contented and comfortable home life.

Here we have a person who would naturally shy away from any situation that he or she saw as boring, though the Water Monkey can be a patient and steadfast supporter of any cause that seems important. This is the natural school governor, is a good parent and a loyal spouse. Some care is necessary with the nervous system, which is not always as strong as seems to be the case. Any tendency for the Water Monkey to exhaust him or her self could eventually lead to a breakdown in general health. Probably the most approachable and loveable member of the Monkey fraternity.

THE WOOD MONKEY

Being allied to the Wood Monkey could mean a certain amount of notoriety, even if the glory that comes your way is of the reflected sort and is mainly down to the versatility of this most fascinating person. The Wood Monkey is truly an original, never at a loss for something to say or do and perhaps the greatest fun to be around of all the Monkey types. The nature is generous and open, though the motivation is towards success and the horizon always looks bright for this character.

If you want to beat the Wood Monkey in an argument you will have to get up very early in the day and not allow your own points to deviate at all. It's probably best not to bother, because the Wood Monkey has the whole discussion sewn up so tight there is little chance of bettering either Miss or Mr in this area of life. All the same the Wood Monkey is a charmer and would certainly prefer not to cross swords with anyone if it is avoidable.

The Wood Monkey is a great servant of society and is often found employed in some capacity which offers the Wood Monkey talent to the betterment of humanity. As a result doctors and nurses are often born under this combination.

Although capable, bright, adept and easy to get on with, the Wood Monkey is inclined to dominate relationships, though manages to do so without being bossy. In its own way this can be terribly infuriating, especially when you realise that you are constantly being duped. The Wood Monkey will simply smile sweetly and announce that your approval has been sought at every turn. It's difficult to argue with this logic and at the end of the day you probably will not want to try. Here we have a character who is basically full of fun.

THE FIRE MONKEY

Many relationships depend upon the fact that people grow into each other with the passage of time. This is especially true when the individuals concerned commence their liaison at an early age. However this is not likely to be much of a possibility if a Fire Monkey forms part of the attachment for this type of person seems to be born what they are and will always want to make the running. The Fire Monkey is a go-getter, is always busy and rarely stops, even to take a breath. As a result both genders born under this combination veer between extreme tension and total exhaustion, a fact that could display itself in terms of ill health later.

Your Fire Monkey is easy to get on with, if you can catch up with him or her long enough to prove the fact. You would certainly never be bored with this character around and would have plenty to talk about, if only you could get him or her to listen.

The Fire Monkey is almost always successful in business and carries a shrewdness that you will not find bettered by any other sign type. Creative, imaginative and full of conflicting impulses, the Fire Monkey wants to be all things to all people all the time. If you can cope with the fact, you might find yourself involved with a really interesting person.

Somewhere along the road though it is good to get to know your partner really well and this possibility cannot be promised with a spouse who is so busy all the time. Protect your Fire Monkey by insisting on plenty of rest and some not so strenuous routines now and again. At least that way they will be around to offer you the passion and intellect of which they are more than capable - if only they will stop running around.

THE EARTH MONKEY

Although very energetic it has to be said that Monkeys are natural thinkers and none more so than the Earth Monkey. This type of person is, in any case, less likely to be running around all the while and will take periods of rest and relaxation which offer time for contemplation too. As a result you will find that you have taken on board the Monkey who achieves the greatest balance of any of this volatile clan.

Earth Monkey types are shrewd, able to feather their own nests and probably yours too, and may turn out to be the best business Monkeys of all. Unlike many of their cousins from other Elements they are not afraid to delegate responsibility and manage to build a wider base for their operations as a result.

Here we find a natural talker, a good friend and a loyal companion, though at the same time someone who remains good to be around and who can be more or less guaranteed to interest you. Although probably not artistic in the general sense of the word Earth Monkey people are creative, and can put this talent to good use in a number of ways.

It is said that Earth Monkeys have all the attributes to make good lovers, but only if they choose less volatile partners than they themselves often turn out to be. Most of this breed remain true to one relationship but will wander if they are discontented or if the support they need is not forthcoming. The way to keep an Earth Monkey happy is to be on hand to talk, to encourage and to help. It might seem that you have a character here who is perpetually willing to help you out of a corner, but a few gestures in the other direction will be appreciated.

THE METAL ROOSTER

Do you want to have your house cleaned, your clothes ironed, your cupboards tidy and your life mapped out days in advance? If the immediate answer to this question is 'yes', then you may choose wisely if you decide to form an alliance with the Metal Rooster. The drawback is that you may also find that you are living with someone who expects a great deal, not only of themselves, but of you too, and it might not be in your power to stand up to the pressures involved.

All Roosters are fairly slow to commit themselves in a relationship sense, though the Metal Rooster is certainly more speedy than the average chicken. Although this individual may not sweep you off your feet, he or she would be more or less certain to sweep your floor and you can be fairly certain of the degree of affection coming your way by the amount that the Metal Rooster is willing to do for you in a practical sense. All the same, this is a chatty character, even if he or she often seems to have nothing especially important to say. In the capability stakes there is nobody better than this most practical of people. Success in business is more or less inevitable and it is fair to say the the Metal Rooster manages to achieve this and yet still always be on hand to sort you out.

Male or female, the Metal Rooster is mother to the whole world and, like the farmyard animal, clucks and fusses about from morning until night. However, this person is very kind, rarely aggressive and is a passionate and imaginative lover, whose stamina knows no bounds. And if this Rooster crows, it is likely to be in praise of you because once you enter his or her life, you are likely to remain there, unless you tend to tire first.

THE WATER ROOSTER

This is a very helpful and a very wily old bird, all things considered, and may turn out to be one of the most personable chickens in the run. Of course a Rooster is a Rooster is a Rooster, and you know right from the start that you have a fuss budget to deal with. Once this fact is understood and accepted, the Water Rooster might not turn out to be such a bad deal.

For a start the Water Rooster is extremely helpful and probably more flexible than most of its cousins. In a practical sense, and especially when it comes to getting things done around the home, the Water Rooster can be more or less guaranteed to be superb. Of course he or she might not do things in quite the way that you would, and will never alter to accommodate your point of view, but at least the work will run smoothly to its conclusion.

The Water Rooster is intelligent can be very charming and will not fuss round you too much in public, which many of the other Rooster types are inclined to do.

There is little impulsiveness about any Rooster, though the Water kind does at least have a degree of originality and a keen sense of humour of the black sort.

What probably sets this type apart significantly lies in the fact that he or she certainly knows their own basic nature very well and can laugh at their own peculiarities. Very few of us can do this and it can be a refreshing complement to any relationship. The Water Rooster has an imagination, of sorts, and will probably be a good lover, just as long as the sheets are clean and aired and the bedroom tidy.

Constancy is more or less certain here and so you may avoid a 'wanderer' in this case.

THE WOOD ROOSTER

This is probably the most comfortable combination of sign and Element as far as the Rooster is concerned and as a result makes for the most comfortable member of the chicken run. However, 'comfortable' for whom? In all probability not for you as the the partner of the Wood Rooster. Although generally cheerful, very capable, tremendously caring and invariably successful, this person has the capacity to drive almost anyone completely up the wall, across the ceiling and down the other side again. Why? Because the Wood Rooster knows how to do everything in the most efficient manner and with the greatest aplomb. The only problem is that you may not have wanted anything doing at all!

Let's face it, when it comes to practicality there is nobody to rival the Wood Rooster, and it turns out to be an even bigger problem that the character not only thinks that he or she is right about everything under the sun - they usually are! Their every look will say 'I told you so' and they will infuriate you all the more by refusing to actually mouth the words. True, you will have a clean house, a spotless car and immaculate children, but will you be really happy?

It takes many different sorts of people to make the world go round, and it's fair to say that the Wood Rooster is one of the most steadfast and reliable people you will ever meet. Relationships are invariably for life and loyalty knows no bounds. There is love of a sort and a depth that most people could never dream of and you will also find a person here who can earn money at the drop of a hat. There is only a particular sort of person for the Wood Rooster. If you are not instinctively drawn to what is written above - look again.

THE FIRE ROOSTER

With the Fire Rooster so much depends on the individual concerned, which is a factor here because no matter what the Element concerned, it is rather difficult for the Rooster type to get away from what he or she is at base. In the case of the Fire Rooster some of the more fussy qualites of the sign tend to be put aside, in favour of a slightly more immediate sort of response to life. This brings a greater sense of fun, slightly better communication skills (as opposed to simply talking 'at' people) and a lessening of the fastidiousness that typifies the Rooster type as a group.

This bird is just as practical as all the rest, though may be slightly more inclined to delegate responsibility, and it is also fair to say the the Fire Rooster would be more likely to go along with your own sensible suggestions, without having to pick the bones out of everything on the way. This person will never be a happy-go-lucky type but does come much nearer to being so than any other type of Rooster. As a bonus you should enjoy the typical loyalty of the sign, together with a good executive ability and a family minded attitude.

It is suggested that the Fire Rooster makes an excellent lover in the physical sense of the word because there is continuity and stamina combined here. Add this to a more open-minded and flexible attitude than other Roosters enjoy and perhaps the rumour concerning the prowess of the Fire Rooster is true. You might really enjoy being around such a person and certainly could not look for a more reliable or consistent partner under most circumstances. Work hard to break down any routines before they become entrenched and who knows? This might be the best sort of Rooster of the lot!

THE EARTH ROOSTER

The Earth Rooster is a person of great charm, who is generally balanced by nature and who is genuinely happy to be what nature made them. This has to be a good thing because there are a great many Rooster types who are far less settled and content than this character turns out to be. To a great extent, what you see is what you get. The Earth Rooster is genuinely less noisy than some of its clucking relatives and is not likely to make a fuss about anything, unless it is the fact that you don't put your clothes away and that you leave the bathroom in a mess.

Here we have a natural homemaker. Usually refined and often a 'cut above the rest', Earth Rooster types are often ribbed at school for being 'swots' or are accused of being 'posh'. In reality there is simply a natural poise and a politeness that many people would suggest that society could do with emulating. Your Earth Rooster will love to throw dinner parties and is fond of a small circle of friends, who often remain pals for life. Unaffected by the ups and downs of life in the way that most people are, a contented Earth Rooster is a joy to behold.

But all that glistens may not be gold. Everything written above is true - as long as things are going the way the Earth Rooster wants them to. This person can nag just as consistently and every bit as forcefully as any Rooster when life does not match its expectations. The Earth Rooster can be fairly materialistic and usually will not settle for anything less than the best.

When in love the Earth Rooster is constant, sincere and quite willing to make a few sacrifices. A paradoxical old bird this one!

THE METAL DOG

A passionate mutt this one and usually a person who is well enough liked by everyone. The Dog is a sociable type, if somewhat intellectually aloof on occasions. All Dogs are natural diplomats and life with the Metal Dog should never be anything less than interesting. Metal Dogs set out to live a busy life and relationships are simply a part of the scenario. If you do not have the full attention of your Metal Dog partner all the time, and this fact bothers you, then it is possible that you have settled on the wrong type of individual in the first place.

Loyalty is a relative commodity to the Dog, though the Metal type is liable to be rather more faithful than average. A deep personal relationship has to be physical, mental and spiritual to keep the Metal Dog happy and the demands that are made of you might seem to be a little unfair at times, particularly since the same sort of commitment in reverse might be rather spasmodic. It could be worth the effort though because this is an entertaining type, with a good sense of humour, a love for the absurd and one of the best sexual imaginations to be found anywhere in the Chinese zoo.

Never expect a simple or uncomplicated life however and be prepared to dash off almost anywhere, probably at a moment's notice.

The Metal Dog is a good worker, if somewhat inclined to change its job on a regular basis, is very subject to boredom and less than willing to consider a tedious routine of any sort. Fun and games are part of the package with this person around and you will not have to look very far to find a good holiday partner, an excellent lover, a diverting cabaret act andr a good, honest friend, all rolled into one.

THE WATER DOG

Oh what a lovely character this is, and how easy it is to fall for the magical touch of this most practised charmer. You probably would not be able to refuse the Water Dog anything, and if this is the case you are in good company because the whole world finds itself at the feet of a person who genuinely has the charm to excel them all. The Water Dog is a natural diplomat and can usually be found smoothing ruffled feathers or bringing some awkward type round to a more sensible point of view.

The Water Dog needs a type of love that others find difficult to offer. There is a deep lack of basic self-confidence which makes for a rather hesitant personal approach, and yet one that is very disarming and quite touching to behold. You never really know where you are with the Water Dog however, since this individual is also quite capable in a day-to-day sense and usually manages to squeeze a fair degree of success from almost any situation.

The Water Dog loves to travel, usually wants a busy social life and may have many friends at a superficial level. Here we have a person who is difficult to know deeply, and one who will probably claim that there is nothing deeper inside them than what shows on the surface.

Don't believe a word of it. The Water Dog is complicated and turns out to be quite a deep thinker. In love he or she is poetical, profound and sincere - at least in a moment-by-moment sense. No matter what the rights and wrongs of the personality or the situation, if you have fallen in love with the Water Dog, nobody has the power to talk you out of it. Simply enjoy what you have.

THE WOOD DOG

What an amiable member of the pack this Dog is, and how easy it would be to fall in love with such a likeable person. In fact it's fair to say with this character that 'what you see is more or less what you get'. Once you get to know the individual concerned there are really few surprises in store, except those that come on every passing day, since the Wood Dog is not a lover of routine and is likely to ring the changes frequently.

A really entertaining soul, the Wood Dog is likely to be a fairly sporting type and enjoys the cut and thrust of life to the full. You won't have to drag him or her out of bed on a morning and arguments within this relationship will be few and far between, unless of course it is you who decides to start them. The Wood Dog is almost universally kind, likes to see the best in everyone and usually comes up trumps when it is important to do so.

Words of love are not hard for this person to find and the Wood Dog will leave you in little doubt concerning their deeper feelings in an emotional sense.

There are always two sides to the see-saw however and it has to be said that the Wood Dog really falls down when it comes to making decisions. Since we have a person here who wants to keep everyone happy, there are occasions when conflict is almost inevitable.

The Wood Dog hates to be disliked and may allow him or her self to be put upon as a result. It's your job to get the Wood Dog out of innumerable scrapes and to be on hand to bandage the emotional hurts that life is apt to dish out from time to time. Chances are that you will be happy to oblige - because that is the sort of person that you are!

THE FIRE DOG

By far the most dynamic member of the Dog pack, the Fire Dog is a person of great charm and character, a habitual talker and a joy to be with most of the time. You would not find life to be at all boring with this sort of individual around and can be fairly certain that he or she will come good regarding any promise that is made to you.

The Fire Dog has one of the best imaginations in the zodiac, though like all Dogs can tend to be a little intellectually aloof if constantly dealing with people who refuse to put their own grey matter to use.

The Fire Dog can get into some terrible scrapes, and as the partner of this type you will be expected to wade in and sort out the situation. Incongruous as it may sometimes seem, the Fire Dog thrives on a life that contains a good deal of conflict, though this critter manages to keep most of it at a distance and could even be accused of allowing others to take the blame for situations that it has personally created. Clearly there is no malice aforethought involved in this process, it's simply that the Fire Dog fails to realise how influential and important it seems to be to others.

When it comes to making waves the Fire Dog is a mid-Atlantic specialist who can then stand back and say, in all sincerity - 'who, me?'

All in all the Fire Dog has far more attributes than failings, is considered by many to be the perfect lover and is always entertaining to be with.

If you want a partner, a lover, a debating society and a deeply revered friend, all rolled into one, get together with the many characters that comprise the Fire Dog.

THE EARTH DOG

This is the idealist of the Dog family and perhaps also the most noble in a general sense. A deeply sensitive character, the Earth Dog is better than all the rest at understanding what makes other people tick and is far less likely to intellectualise situations than many of its cousins. Male and female alike, the Earth Dog has a nurturing tendency, and is always on hand to listen to the problems of the whole world, which it can then invariably sort out with its innate sense of justice and fair play.

Is this individual a paragon then? Unfortunately not, since all sign and Element combinations have positive and negative sides. In fact difficulties coming to the surface with the Earth Dog as part of the scenario could be caused by the selfsame traits that at other times could be called attributes.

This is a hard act to follow, but the Earth Dog will certainly be very unhappy if you are not walking on behind and holding the lead. Your Earth Dog thinks that you have the same revolutionary desire to put the world to rights that he or she possesses and cannot understand if you tire.

It isn't at all easy for most mortals to live with a saint, and that is exactly what it sometimes feels like trying to come to terms within this partnership. Don't worry though. With age comes an understanding that perhaps life is not really all that simple. If this realisation turns to a healthy cynicism then you will find that the Earth Dog is easier to cope with and then all the naturally enjoyable aspects of the person are even more evident.

The Earth Dog loves family life, will adore you and will never, ever really grow up at all. If you can stay young as well - this is a recipe for possible success.

THE METAL PIG

Pigs have the reputation of being deeply sensual people. They are not especially easy to understand and have a side to their nature that is difficult to fathom. In relationships they can be ardent and sincere and none is more so than the Metal Pig. Here we have a personality that combines emotional strength with the subtlety that comes from an 'old soul'.

The Metal Pig has practical skills as well as personal depth and is a born natural when it comes to helping the world as a whole.

It is easy to be awed by the natural fascination of this sign and Element combination and to fall for the magical, poetical approach to life that is invariably present. All the same, this is a difficult person to know fully and you might spend a lifetime reflecting on the surprises that often rise to the surface of the emotional pond. True, you won't be in any doubt about the affection that is generated, or concerning the physical approach to love, which is more noticeable in the case of the Pig than it is in almost any other sign.

The Metal Pig is slightly less sensually motivated than some of its cousins, so you probably will not have to fit an extra bathroom, simply to keep this character happy. Personal success is indicated here and the Metal Pig is a very good provider, an excellent, if somewhat overprotective parent, and a true friend. Loyalty is usually written into the contract though excitement may not be.

This character is steady but is also capable of great intensity. Such people tend to settle down as they grow older and then need to be encouraged not to become couch potatoes. All in all a fairly interesting prospect all the same.

THE WATER PIG

If there is a potential problem with this sort of Pig it probably comes from an individual who is inclined to opt for the wrong sort of relationship early in life and then to regret having done so with the passing of time. This is not the most dynamic Pig and is one that settles for a protective arm, failing to realise its own strengths at first and only coming to terms with them as maturity develops. The Water Pig is a great lover of luxury, can be guaranteed to spend hours preening him or her self and is by far and away the most fastidious Pig of them all.

The Water Pig loves genuinely and deeply. It will sacrifice almost anything to make situations work out as it believes they should and is likely to devote a great percentage of life to nurturing and encouraging a family, which will be more important to it than anything else.

This variety of Pig is emotionally responsive, though deep and difficult to understand fully. Part of the reason for this is that such people do not know themselves all that well and are, in any case, fairly lacking in personal confidence much of the time. Water Pigs can be very secretive and like to keep their own inner souls locked away.

You may first recognise this person via the sultry good looks which are often present. This is a truly sexy Pig and is unlikely to go short of admirers, many of whom would gladly risk all to possess such a fascinating person. But here is a problem, because people generally do want to own the Water Pig. At first this seems fine, but eventually this person will react and this fact itself can lead to difficulties.

A good and realistic start to any relationship is vital in this instance.

THE WOOD PIG

Another sympathetic Pig this one, or would empathy be a better word for the natural reactions of the Wood Pig? In most cases this is so and many individuals would relate that this fact alone makes the Wood Pig good to be with and in many respects the ideal partner. The Wood Pig is kind, loving, capable of great insight and probably more stable than some of its counterparts. There is a natural practicality and an ability to get things right which is not always typical of the Pig as a type. The Wood Pig wants to help the world and tends to do so with imagination and enthusiasm.

There is an ability here to create a loving environment, which is useful when difficulties arise, because the basis of the Wood Pig's motivation is towards stability. Part of this might be because Mr or Miss Wood Pig understands the depths of their own nature and deals with potential problems thrown up by it.

There is certainly more humour here and an ability to adapt cheerfully to most of the eventualities that life throws up. The Wood Pig is also co-operative and knows that the best way to success in a relationship is via compromise, something that many Pig types seem to singularly ignore.

The Wood Pig is fond of luxury and can lounge for hours in warm and comfortable surroundings, and though by no means a slouch when it comes to getting things done, this might be the least physically motivated Pig in the pen. Not that this turns out to be the case in a personal clinch because the Wood Pig was born to enjoy sexual relationships, which it sees as an extension of the sensuality it understands so well. It is true that some Wood Pigs can be a little selfish on occasions.

THE FIRE PIG

Certainly not the easiest Pig to understand, mainly because the strength of the Fire Element is inclined to work in a very different manner to the general trends of the Pig as a type. This is clearly a person to be reckoned with but one who is so deep that you would need a very long rope indeed to get to the bottom of this nature. Right from the start it might be best to advise that you do not really try to do so.

Most of the individuals who live happily with the Fire Pig, of which there are many, do so from a position of accepting, rather than analysing.

The Fire Pig is quite capable of achieving great success in life, and this applies every bit as much to relationships as it does to work.

Here we find a sympathetic person, but one who is able to translate a desire to be on the side of others into a genuine ability to change circumstances on their behalf. This is especially true in the case of a loving relationship because the Fire Pig is a staunch supporter of partner and family and would gladly sacrifice almost anything on their behalf.

You may find the Fire Pig to be a little bossy, but he or she is also magnetic, alluring, sexy and quite different from almost any other type of person.

There is the fascination of a magician here and an ability to turn almost any sort of situation to advantage. Love or hate this person, you cannot ignore them. Life may not always be easy, but is almost certain to be interesting in a thousand different ways. That is why the individual who has lived for any length of time with a Fire Pig could probably settle for nothing less!

THE EARTH PIG

This has to be one of happiest Pigs of the lot, if only because all Pigs love to be in, or near, the earth. Don't forget that Pig types as a group are rank sensualists, and this is never better catered for than when Earth is the Element on offer. Not that this is the most outwardly dynamic member of the Pig family. Here we have a low-key sort of person, and one who will not shout the odds unless it is absolutely necessary to do so. The Earth Pig is acquisitive, anxious to please, can be very friendly and would do anything for someone who is held dear.

Probably the best family Pig, the Earth type usually wants to find a suitable partner and to settle down as early as possible. From this point on a great deal of the incentive for living is pushed in the direction of those who are closest in a family sense.

The Earth Pig should not be allowed to settle down too much however, since to do so is not all that good for this sign and Element combination. Earth Pigs need to keep on the move, to have a number of different interests in life and to enjoy a flexible routine.

No prospective partner would find it all that difficult to get the Earth Pig into bed, though it might be rather harder to get them out again. The Earth Pig is the greatest sensualist of the lot and loves luxury in all its forms.

A settled sort of life is the prognosis here, whilst multiple relationships for the Earth Pig are very rare. A single-minded type of person all the same and certainly not the sort who would suit every prospective partner. What really counts is persuading the Earth Pig that there is an interesting world beyond the garden gate.

CHINESE ASCENDANTS AND LOVE

The Earth turns on its axis all the time, and it looks from our point of view as if the sky is passing over our heads. The belt of stars that the ancients set aside as being the most responsive to human beings, and the world at large, is called the zodiac. Part of this is therefore passing over our heads all the time. The segment of the zodiac that is passing over the Western horizon when you are born is called the 'Ascendant' and this has a great bearing on the sort of person you turn out to be.

In the West, working out the Ascendant is a tricky business, but the efficient Chinese managed to work out a system which is very much easier to use. You can work out your own Chinese Ascendant, or that of anyone you know, simply by referring to the table that appears on the following page. You simply have to look up a time of birth and read to the right of this to discover what the relevant Chinese sign is. The readings for all the Ascendants follow the charts and you can then see how this meshes with the information you have already gleaned from the Chinese Year Sign. Bear in mind that there could be a few contradictions, but then that is part of what life is about.

Gradually you are building up a better and better picture, either of yourself, or of some other individual in whom you have a particular interest. As far as the Ascendant is concerned, its strength or weakness in the nature of any person depends upon how dominant it is, relative to other qualities that you have already discovered. One thing is certain though - somewhere along the line you will notice the influence of any Chinese Ascendant.

COMPARISON CHART

I am always being asked how Chinese Astrology relates to the branch of the subject most common in the West, and there is a very real relationship between the two alternatives. Every Chinese sign has a Western counterpart and although there are slight differences, in the main the characteristics of the comparisons are sound. The second table on the following page allows you to discover, quickly, just what Chinese sign relates to its more commonly understood Western counterpart.

CHINESE ASCENDANT TABLE

HOUR OF BIRTH	SIGN	HOUR OF BIRTH	SIGN
1am. to 2am.	OX	2am. to 3am.	OX
3am. to 4am.	TIGER	4am. to 5am.	TIGER
5am. to 6am.	RABBIT	6am. to 7am.	RABBIT
7am. to 8am.	DRAGON	8am. to 9am.	DRAGON
9am. to 10am.	SNAKE	10am. to 11am.	SNAKE
11am. to 12am.	HORSE	12am. to 1pm.	HORSE
1pm. to 2pm.	GOAT	2pm. to 3pm.	GOAT
3pm. to 4pm.	MONKEY	4pm. to 5pm.	MONKEY
5pm. to 6pm.	ROOSTER	6pm. to 7pm.	ROOSTER
7pm. to 8pm.	DOG	8pm. to 9pm.	DOG
9pm. to 10pm.	PIG	10pm. to 11pm.	PIG
11pm. to 12pm.	RAT	12pm. to 1am.	RAT

CHINESE SIGNS AND WESTERN COUNTERPARTS

CHINESE SIGN	WESTERN SIGN
DRAGON	ARIES
SNAKE	TAURUS
HORSE	GEMINI
GOAT	CANCER
MONKEY	LEO
ROOSTER	VIRGO
DOG	LIBRA
PIG	SCORPIO
RAT	SAGITTARIUS
OX	CAPRICORN
TIGER	AQUARIUS
RABBIT	PISCES

THE RAT ASCENDANT AND LOVE

A fact that certainly cannot be denied is the dynamic quality of the Rat nature, which shows itself in every sphere of life and never more so than in the case of love.

Whatever the other Chinese astrological associations the person with a Rat Ascendant is bound to be a real charmer and a good personality to know. The attitude towards life is one that makes for a person who will always want to join in any fun that is around, as well as to make a great deal more on his or her own account. You may find this type to be rather complex, but at least when any difficulties do arise, they are not likely to last very long. The Rat Ascendant brings a potential for material success but this might tend to be of a stop-start nature and sometimes gives the impression of a 'fly-by-night' sort of character. In reality this is not the case and most Rat Ascendant types are basically honest and decent.

Life with this person is certainly not always easy, but you should usually find it to be interesting and there will be no shortage of hearts and flowers. The Rat is a kind-hearted type and a genuine believer in equality, that is as long as you show that you can stand up for yourself and therefore deserve the Rat's respect.

Don't expect to get all your own way because this is certainly not the way that things are likely to turn out. All the same you should find that travel is likely, and many changes of scene in your life as a whole. The Rat Ascendant type is a good, if somewhat unorthodox sort of person, who is always willing to allow children to find themselves naturally. This individual is bound to be different, but it is probably the differences that attract you in any case.

THE OX ASCENDANT AND LOVE

Life with the Ox Ascendant person is bound to be a little tedious from time to time, unless you care for the plodding, methodical quality of this sort of individual. Of course much depends on the the other Chinese signs involved but the part that the Ox has to play in the nature is almost certain to show at one level or another.

Here we have a person who is very reliable, rarely likely to take unnecessary chances and who is likely to do quite well in financial terms, though probably across a number of years. You won't always be happy with having to wait and yet the Ox Ascendant usually does win out in the end. The patience shown on the way could turn out to be an object lesson to almost anyone.

It isn't hard to keep on the right side of the Ox Ascendant, who is a generally likeable and fairly easygoing type. The only time you might experience any real sort of difficulty would be if you chose to push the Ox into a corner. In reality this is probably the best fighter anywhere in the Chinese zoo and represents someone who will never back down on those occasions when he or she feels that they have right on their side. There is patience here in abundance, a love for a peaceful life and a recognition of responsibility that is probably second to none.

You will always know exactly where you are if you decide to settle down with an Ox Ascendant type, though you might forego some of the excitement that comes along with other sign types. However, times change, and the Ox Ascendant can too, that is if you have a century or two to work on them and the true patience of a saint yourself!

THE TIGER ASCENDANT AND LOVE

A large part of love is being able to live with the person in question, which although always an adventure with a Tiger Ascendant type could not always be described as easy. Here we have a person who is basically a loner, though of course other aspects of the astrological nature have to be considered carefully too. Tiger types are intellectually aloof and are usually good talkers; they don't give in easily when they think they have right on their side and yet are usually quite fair-minded and willing to give others the benefit of the doubt.

You probably will not find yourself facing a jealous sort of partner and, if anything, the situation is rather likely to be reversed, for the Tiger Ascendant is inclined to wander if he or she is not entirely happy with the way things are in an established relationship. The way to avoid this is to recognise what interests this character, and to be willing to go along with it. On the way there are gains of all kinds, not least of all the interest of coming to terms with someone who seems capable of representing something different on every passing day.

Tiger Ascendant types like to have a good time, but they can usually be persuaded to settle down in the end and are good family members with a great sense of responsibility. However this does not mean that they will want to lose their independence on the way and they do have rather revolutionary ideas when it comes to rearing children. The Tiger type can keep a sense of proportion, the only real problem here being that the proportions tend to change rather a lot, so that it is sometimes difficult to know what is expected of you.

Stay flexible and enjoy the gains that come from this unique and refreshing type.

THE RABBIT ASCENDANT AND LOVE

The Rabbit side of any individual could easily be swamped if some of the other astrological qualities are of a much more dominant type, though somewhere, deep in the nature, there is a love of peace and harmony that is certain to show through.

The Rabbit is a difficult character to fathom, but one who is usually very pleasant and who wants to see the other person's point of view at all costs. There is great warmth and sincerity here, not to mention the ability and the desire to work on behalf of others for considerable periods of time. The Rabbit Ascendant wants to help the whole world, which is why you might lose out on occasion because nobody can do everything - even though this person is apt to try.

If you want affection look no further than this direction because any Rabbit type will offer this in abundance. All the same this can be a hard act to follow because, without intending to be so, the Rabbit Ascendant could be rather possessive and is sometimes a little constraining. All the same this is an easy person to love and one who would not willingly let you down or cause problems in your life.

The potential family-wise is particularly good since the Rabbit Ascendant type usually makes an extremely good parent and provider, whilst at the same time never losing the potential to be an ideal lover and a true friend. Most people like the Rabbit, as much as anything because there is so little to dislike. Of course this might not make for the most exciting person in the world, though the Rabbit is adaptable and will often be willing to take the lead from you.

Keep an open mind and make certain that you know what other Chinese animals are at work in this nature.

THE DRAGON ASCENDANT AND LOVE

Get out the safety net and prepare yourself for a life that is every bit as interesting, colourful and sometimes as demanding as the circus. It doesn't matter what else is at work here astrologically, the dynamism of the Dragon Ascendant is bound to play its part in this nature. You need enthusiasm, energy and a strong will of your own to make the best of this type, though it must be said from the outset that the rewards for your effort are likely to be very high indeed.

Dragon types are go-getters and if you want the best out of life you must be willing to take the same express train to success that they choose for themselves. This could mean a frequent change of address and in extreme cases might also indicate a different country. There are no limits to the imagination of this individual and you can expect to be bullied a little - that is unless you are willing to stick up for yourself. The Dragon Ascendant is usually fair and respects you better if you express a particular point of view under any given circumstance.

Routines are a bore to this man or woman and are not usually tolerated at all if there is any alternative. Here we have one who is used to giving orders rather than taking them, a fact that can be just as relevant in relationships as it is in any other sphere of life. There is good concentration, a concern for relatives and friends and every possible form of intelligence that nature could bestow. It's a fast-track ride and no mistake, though to some this sort of person is meat and drink. A calmer year sign or Moon position will not radically alter the Dragon characteristics, because the Dragon usually predominates over everything.

THE SNAKE ASCENDANT AND LOVE

The Snake is a lover of peace and order and is usually to be found in the expected place, which is so curled up in a corner sleeping! But in a way this is not fair because the Snake Ascendant type is a hard worker, even if he or she does know full well how to relax when the opportunity presents itself.

To call this person lazy would be a distortion of the truth, though if you want to be swept off your feet in the dazzle of romance you might have a fairly protracted wait. For the most part you will be expected to make much of the running and this is an aspect of life with the Snake type that can sometimes prove to be a little frustrating.

It all depends on what sort of a person you are yourself, but you should never run away with the idea that the Snake is incapable of love. In fact the reverse is true because many would believe that there is not a more faithful or attentive partner to be found anywhere.

Everything is solid about the Snake Ascendant, and this probably includes the body too, because such types are sensualists in every sense of the word. Of course this also includes a love of sex and a good imagination concerning the mechanics of the business. You can expect a stable sort of life, and travel may not feature all that heavily unless you are the one who goes down the High Street to book the tickets.

To some, this person is the ideal partner and you can be certain that a Snake Ascendant would take the hard edge off more dynamic astrological components. Too much Snake in any nature is not a good thing, however, and is a recipe for getting out the hammock and being prepared to laze around in the sunshine too.

THE HORSE ASCENDANT AND LOVE

Oh what a wonderful thing life with the Horse Ascendant individual can be - but oh what a disaster if things don't go according to plan. To be perfectly honest there rarely is any sort of plan at all, and this is where any real problems begin. The Horse type always means well and is one of the most charming types you will ever meet, but the word commitment probably does not appear in the Horse vocabulary at all, which is not likely to suit all potential partners.

Things usually get done, even if it is invariably just in the nick of time and there is always plenty of social potential on offer.

As far as routines are concerned, well, the Horse Ascendant will not prevent you from dealing with as many of them as you wish, but he or she simply refuses to join in. Not that the Horse is incapable of doing any work - just absent for so much of the time.

The Horse is easy to love and turns out to be one of the most endearing characters that one could ever meet. The Horse can be forgiven anything, if only because there is no malice whatsoever in this most infuriating yet most fascinating type.

When it comes to family life the Horse really comes into his or her own. As a parent the Horse Ascendant is tolerant, and usually joins in all the antics of the children, probably because he or she never grew up in the first place.

The Horse Ascendant type is a good and imaginative lover, usually contrives to have no money but can make a little go a long way. This is a confusing character, yet one of the most charismatic people you are ever going to be honoured to know. A person to love and to hold - if you can. Not an easy prospect for many.

THE GOAT ASCENDANT AND LOVE

If it is a combination of love, reliability and practical skill that you are looking for in life, it could be that the Goat Ascendant will be right up your street. This person is considerate, often quiet by nature, tolerant, adaptable and kind. Goat Ascendants make good friends as well as excellent romantic partners and will usually go to great lengths to protect and nurture family members.

Perhaps this person is not the most exciting type you will ever meet, yet being adaptable by nature, the Goat is likely to adopt a fair percentage of your views of life. Actually this turns out to be a superficial illusion because the Goat Ascendant is really quite deep, so that unless you are willing to probe very carefully, you may never get to know what makes him or her tick at all.

In family terms there is certainly not a better sign, and the Goat Ascendant, male or female, is a natural homemaker. Parenting comes as second nature and you should discover that no matter how good you are at dealing with little ones, the Goat is better. This in itself could turn out to be a slight problem for some, because here we have a person who is genuinely good at almost anything he or she chooses to turn their hands to.

Being naturally creative the Goat can make a silk purse out of a sow's ear, and still make a stew from what remains.

Goats are good and capable workers and bring home the bacon consistently. They will tolerate almost anything for a season, but do have a point beyond which they will not be pushed. As long as this fact is taken on board and the Goat Ascendant type is treated with the respect that is deserved, all should be well.

THE MONKEY ASCENDANT AND LOVE

An ingenious, fascinating and quite capable person, the Monkey Ascendant type is good to know, fun to be with and quite certain to cheer up your life no end. The Monkey type is loyal and endearing, romantic by nature and only a little lazy on occasions. You cannot underestimate the potential of this individual when it comes to earning money and you should find that you are always number one as the Monkey's partner.

The Monkey is not one to be put upon and will invariably spend time sorting out his or her own personal lot in life, which means a busy person who may not be at home quite as much as you might wish. The only way to deal with this situation is probably to accept it, since it is impossible to change the Monkey or create an alternative person, no matter how much better it would suit you to be able to do so.

The creative potential here is good, particularly when it comes to inventing ideas that make life more interesting and stimulating. What is more the Monkey will always be willing to take you along for the ride and may whisk you off to almost any part of the globe at the drop of a hat.

Although the Monkey Ascendant is reliable, he or she may not turn out to be exactly predictable, and this is part of the spice that makes life well worth living. From one day to the next you might not know what sort of surprise is on the way and unless you are the type of person who requires an absolutely static sort of existence, the Monkey attitude to life should prove to be enthralling.

The Monkey has a strong sex drive, but this is displayed via a very romantic and often poetic attitude, so that feeling warm and protected is not hard. The Monkey tends to be very original, which makes for an interesting life.

THE ROOSTER ASCENDANT AND LOVE

The Rooster is a fastidious type, so unless other aspects of the individual you are looking at come from different parts of the Chinese zodiac, you may not find this individual all that easy to live with. True, there is great commitment here, and a sense of responsibility that is second to none, and yet the Rooster Ascendant can bring a level of care that some people would relate to as being plain boring.

This person shows a great tendency to worry about things, and goes around the farmyard of life clucking and scratching everything, if only to try and overturn potential problems before they even arise. Because this puts you on the receiving end, unless you recognise the Rooster for the deeply concerned person that he or she genuinely is, you are certain to tire of the constant fuss about nothing. So much is this the case with the Rooster Ascendant that we find here a potential to be over-cautious, pessimistic and pedantic. This might not be your cup of tea at all, and especially not if your own nature runs quite contrary to this tendency.

Realising just how loving, kind and helpful this person can be could redress the balance a little and you certainly could not find a more concerned type than that which the Rooster Ascendant represents. Some of the less favourable traits can be modified, or even changed, with time and patience, and it really depends on just how patient you are yourself. The Rooster Ascendant type is a considerate lover, a good provider and probably also something of a health freak. He or she will put a protective arm around your shoulder that is more convincing than that coming from any other Chinese sign, but can you really cope with life in the clucking, strutting chicken-run for most of the time?

THE DOG ASCENDANT AND LOVE

The Dog is difficult to dislike, under almost any circumstances, since here we have an Ascendant that bestows great kindness, understanding and patience. The Dog Ascendant type is rarely careful, always interesting and usually intelligent. However, there are two sides to every coin and so some care is necessary before you think that you have scooped the pool and throw in your lot with this type.

Although possessed of great charm, there is a certain degree of uncertainty with this sign and you may not always know exactly where your Dog Ascendant is likely to be at any given time.

The Dog is also fairly unpredictable and so you can never really be certain how this type will react under any given circumstance.

The Dog Ascendant type has good executive ability and you should feel quite well blessed most of the time by the words of love that come so easily and are readily pushed in your direction. For example, if the Dog type actually manages to remember when your birthday is, then you can expect to have breakfast in bed and to be spoiled all day long.

The Dog Ascendant person has a good imagination and will express this in sexual terms, via a sex drive that some would see as second to none. And although we find a person here who may not be the most faithful, as long as things are going well and boredom does not set in, this should not be a problem. You may not have to ring the changes yourself, since the Dog is quite ready and able to do this for you. All that is required of you is the ability to turn your world upside down at a moment's notice and to be willing to go along with some of the most hairbrained schemes you have ever encountered.

THE PIG ASCENDANT AND LOVE

This is not the easiest person in the world to understand and so much depends on what other Chinese associations exist within the nature if you want to assess how the Pig Ascendant is likely to respond to love and life. In most cases the Pig Ascendant has a fairly sensual approach to life and so he or she is often to be found eating, bathing, sleeping or making love. However, all of this comes further down the road than the practical aspects of life and it is true to say that the Pig is a good worker, an excellent provider and a great believer in family life.

A slight word of caution could be a little jealousy, which can show with either sex. True, it's not of the type that would make you feel bad about simply setting off for the shops on your own, but this individual will not be too happy about deep relationships you may form outside of your romantic attachment with them. Perhaps to make up for this shortcoming, the Pig Ascendant will love you deeply, cherish you constantly and is likely to remain faithful through thick and thin.

Always be on your alert when it comes to diet, or you could end up with a fat piggy sharing your life and your bed, and try to make regular, healthy exercise part of your family routine. The Pig Ascendant will go along with this, if a little reluctantly at first, but since this is a person who can readily adopt a habit, it should eventually come as second nature.

There is a great desire to please at the heart of all Pig types, even if they sometimes have a rather odd way of displaying the fact.

And don't forget - Pig people are very good at making money.

LOVE AND COMPATIBILITY

In all forms of astrology it is useful to know what signs of the zodiac your own birth sign is likely to get along with. The Chinese are no exception in this regard, and especially where love is concerned, have always been careful to look at the way other signs relate to their own. Of course it makes sense to also bear in mind the Ascendant and Moon Sign when assessing the chances of any two people hitting it off.

Below you will find a chart which makes it simple for you to find the comparison between any two Chinese signs, Look for one sign down the left-hand side of the chart, and the sign you want to compare it with along the top. Where the two coincide you will see a page number, Turn to that page in the following section to learn about Chinese Animal compatibility.

	RAT	OX	TIG	RAB	DRA	SNA	HOR	GOA	MON	ROO	DOG	PIG
RAT	158	158	158	159	159	159	160	160	160	161	161	161
OX	158	162	162	162	163	163	163	164	164	164	165	165
TIG	158	162	165	166	166	166	167	167	167	168	168	168
RAB	159	162	166	169	169	169	170	170	170	171	171	171
DRA	159	163	166	169	172	172	172	173	173	173	174	174
SNA	159	163	166	169	172	174	175	175	175	176	176	176
HOR	160	163	167	170	172	175	177	177	177	178	178	178
GOA	160	164	167	170	173	175	177	179	179	179	180	180
MON	160	164	167	170	173	175	177	179	180	181	181	181
ROO	161	164	168	171	173	176	178	179	181	182	182	182
DOG	161	165	168	171	174	176	178	180	181	182	183	183
PIG	161	165	168	171	174	176	178	180	181	182	183	183

RAT AND RAT

The Rat is naturally a fairly volatile character, so two of them together can be quite a combination. There are certain to be many sparks flying here and the parties concerned will need to display a high level of patience and understanding if things are to work out well. As with all identical signs you should expect to find a meeting of minds and an intellectual understanding that adds zest to the relationship. There should also be a good degree of sexual union, since the imagination and aspirations of two Rats together will allow a high degree of fun once the lights are switched out - or more likely in this case - left on! Quite a possibility this, but not always easy.

RAT AND OX

A good combination from the point of view of the Ox, though in some ways probably less so in the case of the Rat. Rat types need a constant stream of conversation, interest and even excitement in order to feel that life is rewarding, whereas these qualities do not come naturally to the more steady Ox. To compensate, the solid Ox could create greater potential for success in the case of the Rat and might bring a degree of stability that would otherwise be missing. At a deeply personal level the staying power of the Ox meets the imagination of the Rat, and this can make for a most interesting sex life.

RAT AND TIGER

If there is a problem here, it certainly does not stem from any lack of excitement or action. What really might be difficult is the fact that both the Rat and the Tiger are by nature individualists, and although the Rat is probably the more sociable of the two, both parties here want to have their own way. This could lead to some very lively rows and although the Tiger might work through these positively, the Rat could easily tire and wander off to look for something better. Not the highest marks here it's true, but there are exceptions that prove every rule and this could be one of them. A good start is most important, and plenty of patience too!

RAT AND RABBIT

Few people could fail to love the Rabbit, who is a mild-mannered and very likeable type. The Rat is no exception, but might tend to dominate the relationship unless the Rat concerned is very intelligent and knows him or her self really well. Not that this needs to be a bad thing in any case, because there are Rabbit types who genuinely do want a strong shoulder to lean on. The Rat can provide this, but on the other hand may not be as reliable as a Rabbit partner would wish. There are plenty of marks here for potential success, but the realities of life might tell a different story. All the same, there are many examples of this combination that do work.

RAT AND DRAGON

There is great potential for success here, though it might be of the more volatile sort and everything really depends on whether the relationship manages to get past the initial stages. Dragon people are very dominant and tend to rule the roost most of the time. This is not always good for them and it might be fair to suggest that the Rat is the only sign that can hold its own in a struggle for power. Dragons are always dynamic but are not so clever as the wily Rat, and they could constantly find themselves hoodwinked into compromise. Once the ground rules are sorted, the Dragon will develop respect for the Rat.

RAT AND SNAKE

Rats are always on the go, in fact no Chinese sign is more inclined to keep running around the maze of life. The Snake, on the other hand, simply refuses to be rushed into anything. If there is a problem with this union then look towards this very different approach to life in order to find it. The sensual potential of the Snake may hypnotise the Rat, though probably not indefinitely, and if any partner is going to become bored with this combination, it is likely to be the Rat. Probably not a great potential for success, but there could be a great deal of interest on the way. In all probability the Rat and the Snake would not be mutually attracted in the first place.

RAT AND HORSE

Although these two signs are astrological opposites, they have so much in common that ultimate success and happiness certainly could not be ruled out in this case. Both signs are looking for an interesting and exciting sort of life and there is a shared intellectual capacity that would send shocks of fascination back and forth between the two. There might be a constant game of tig, and the potential for faithfulness may not be all that wonderful, yet the two parties could keep coming back because they have so much to gain from each other. Light the blue touch paper and stand back. This could just turn out to be a happier match than almost anyone would imagine.

RAT AND GOAT

There must be examples of this combination proving to be happy and successful, but there are almost certainly many more instances when it does not. The Goat wants a peaceful life, which the Rat is not likely to supply, whereas the Rat needs constant excitement, which the Goat experiences in different surroundings and under alternative circumstances. True, the Goat can be fairly intrepid, but does not respond to the social stimulus which is so much a part of the Rat scene. All in all it does not seem likely that the Rat and the Goat would find too much in the way of common ground .

RAT AND MONKEY

The Rat and the Monkey have one very important quality in common, in addition to a host of others. At heart, both these types have a very strong ego and tend to like themselves. Since both are also very good at handing out compliments, we might find a mutual appreciation society in the offing that works in so many directions it makes the situation look like a cat's cradle. This potential deserves full marks, even if neither sign is especially faithful or particularly deep by nature. The home would be ostentatious and there may be significant wealth, since both partners have good earning potential. On the other hand this might be a combination of hippy types.

RAT AND ROOSTER

The average Rooster might well drive the average Rat up the wall, whilst in the opposite direction the poor Rooster would never know where he or she is within the relationship. Much depends on the genders involved, because female Roosters are not generally interested in considering themselves particularly liberated and could go to great lengths to make a male Rat feel comfortable. Rules and regulations get on the nerves of the Rat, whilst the Rooster must have them in order to live a contented life. Male Rooster versus female Rat is rarely likely to work and could lead to some very unhealthy and acrimonious rows. Even the reverse situation is not without its ups and downs.

RAT AND DOG

The Dog is so easy to get on with that the affable Rat is likely to be drawn in this direction almost instinctively. Dog types can live happily with almost any other sign, though from the point of view of the Rat, this might be the most rewarding combination possible. Most Dog people are willing to adapt and to fall in line with what is going on around them, but they are lovers of adventure and excitement, which is exactly what the Rat is capable of supplying. At a personal level this could turn out to be one of the most exciting combinations possible and it is unlikely that there would be any sudden reversals.

RAT AND PIG

If there is a problem here it stems from the fact that the Rat and the Pig are basically so different. Of course, as we have seen, opposites can attract, but probably will not do so readily in this instance. Of course both these signs are basically reasonable, so that as flatmates they would probably get on very well, which makes this a good combination for friendship, but less so romantically. The Rat is a clever type and probably too much so for the deeper and more sensitive Pig. Whichever part of this combination you represent, you might well find yourself drinking at the same bar as your opposite, but would most likely be quite happy to leave things at this level.

OX AND OX

There is a good potential within this relationship, unless of course the two people concerned tend to drive each other up the wall. The potential problem lies in the fact that the Ox is a very steady sort of person, so that two of them together could lead to a very sedentary sort of life, which might suit both, or in the end neither. Rewards come in a material sense, since the Ox type is a good earner and a responsible saver. All the same there does need to be an input of excitement in any personal relationship and this might be missing with this combination.

As long as both individuals recognise this fact and are willing to deal with it, all might be well.

OX AND TIGER

The Tiger is a character with great get-up-and-go, and if only for this reason the Ox and Tiger combination could turn out to be a very good one. Whilst the Tiger pushes matters forward all the time, the Ox provides a stable and steady platform on which to base the relationship. Ox people can tend to take life seriously, which the Tiger rarely does, and so the alchemical mixing which typifies the best of relationships is clearly possible here. Both the practical aspects of life and the more personal ones are apt to work out well and there is a fairly instinctive understanding that often emerges when opposites such as these come together.

OX AND RABBIT

Even if this relationship does not turn out to be what both parties expect it to be, it seems most unlikely that either partner would be willing to actually say anything and the reason for this state of affairs lies in the very kind nature of both parties. There is unlikely to be any sort of argument and life could jog along in a steady and a positive way. The truth is that there may be a slight lack of passion, but even this may not get in the way of the form of idyllic happiness that is possible. A happy home is the usual end product, filled with a special sort of love and probably many children. One of the best combinations for both animal types.

OX AND DRAGON

It is obvious that the Dragon is a very dynamic type and might tend to intimidate the much quieter Ox a little at first. Although this might seem to be a fairly ideal sort of match there are drawbacks, probably because the Dragon is a pusher, whilst the Ox refuses to budge unless it wants to. As a result we could find a stalemate cropping up and a few pregnant silences developing. Dragons do like to be looked after, and there is nobody around better than the Ox for being able to supply the basic needs of life. Amongst relationships generally this one stands a fair chance, though probably not in the case of the most stubborn of Ox types.

OX AND SNAKE

This has the makings of a steady relationship but certainly not one of the more exciting variety. All the same, it should suit both parties fairly well and is the basis for a kind of happiness that some combinations never achieve. There is likely to be a tidy home, a happy family and a very sedate way of going on. Look for this pair in the winter, and they will be toasting their toes by the fire. Seek them in the summer and you might find them laying side by side in a hammock. Few battles would ensue and on the whole there is a hard-working but much resting balance that many would envy. Probably a good scenario for material success in the fullness of time.

OX AND HORSE

Some Ox types do need the sort of excitement that a Horse person can easily bring into their lives. Not that the poor bovine would always realise the fact and the Ox in this situation could find him or her self involved in a whirlwind of activity that is certainly not second nature. After a while things should settle down, in so far as any household containing a Horse person could, though the life of the Ox involved in this relationship is never going to be quite the same again. But these are natural opposites and might do each other a great deal of good, since the shortcomings of each will be met by the good points of the other. In the main a good prospect.

OX AND GOAT

If this attachment is going to work out well, it will not be on the strength of the natural talkative nature of either individual and could lead to a very quiet sort of household indeed. Both Ox and Goat are basically shy types at heart and although something might be achieved on a practical level, there would not be much in the way of intellectual stimulation to lift the union. All the same, things would happen in this household, because both types are able to turn their hand to almost any routine task. There might also be moments of extreme passion, since the Ox and Goat are both very sexually motivated. It's hard to see how these two might come together in the first place however.

OX AND MONKEY

Ox types do not care for being forced into any situation that goes against the grain, whilst the Monkey never gives up when it comes to making an individual do exactly what they wish. As a result there could be some very immediate problems here which would prevent this seed from germinating in the first place. The Monkey can be quite selfish in its own way, but then so is the Ox, but from a very different set of values and motivations. It would never be possible to say that any combination can be ruled out, but circumstances work against this one, if both characters are true to their metal.

OX AND ROOSTER

Anyone entering a household set up by an Ox and a Rooster would find a well-ordered and neat sort of environment and one that would know much in the way of personal happiness. There is an instinctive understanding possible in this case, which is more than strong enough to take care of any minor difficulties that might arise. The Ox is neat and methodical, which suits the more fussy but equally fastidious Rooster down to the ground. Roosters can be chatty, which would force the Ox to communicate more than it might otherwise. Family life would be settled and although travel might be limited, happiness may not be.

OX AND DOG

Dogs are adaptable, of this there is no doubt at all. This fact alone may go part of the way to explaining the success that is possible with this union. The same could not be said of the Ox however, so most of the giving, shifting and ultimate changing necessary would certainly have to come from the direction of the patient and loveable Dog. All the same, the Ox would be nefit from the happy-go-lucky attitude of this sort of partner and as a result could find a higher degree of sparkle within him or herself. There is a sort of mutual melting to this union, where both parties gain greatly from the strong points of the other in the fullness of time.

OX AND PIG

There can be little doubt that any initial attachment here comes as a result of physical attraction and a common love of sensuality, which is second nature to both animal types. Once the relationship has begun it is doubtful if this couple would be seen out in the street much and might be found in the bedroom more often than not. Both love to eat, to sleep, to bathe and to make love, so there is no lack of common interests to keep this relationship alive and kicking. Sooner or later someone is going to have to introduce this pair to abstinence, after which a state of near normality might prevail and other mutually enjoyed aspects of life could be explored.

TIGER AND TIGER

There is some truth in the adage that 'The Tiger walks alone', and that might make this pairing a little unlikely. It's fair to say that coming together with a person of one's own type is not uncommon, but where this does happen there has to be a fairly good estimation of self-worth in the first place. Since the Tiger is often confused about him or her self, he or she could hardly be expected to instinctively recognise the potential in another of the same breed. If these initial barriers can be broken down however, this is an intellectual and interesting possibility for both parties concerned. The matching is unusual, but magnetic and compulsive to the outsider.

TIGER AND RABBIT

Since the Tiger is not the most easy person in the world to understand, the Rabbit stands the chance of coming out of this union as the loser, no matter how hard he or she works to establish a consistent rapport with this most unusual of signs. But for all, this might prove to be a good match in the long run, since both signs are basically kind and at least do try to be understanding. The home would be a little 'odd' when viewed from the perspective of the outsider because the unique qualities of the Tiger would bring out the individualist in the Rabbit too. A few arguments would be likely but these would invariably turn out to be a storm in a teacup.

TIGER AND DRAGON

There is a great natural attraction in this case, probably born of a mutual respect for a partner of equal merit and potential power. What the Dragon can manage physically the Tiger can meet and often defeat on an intellectual level. On the way there would be some fiery and quite acrimonious exchanges, but probably a love that knows a depth that few ever really fathom. If either party is looking for a truly easy life, they would not go down this road in the first place, though since neither the Tiger nor the Dragon wants to be bored, the challenge is probably a good one. Attitude is all-important in this union and somewhere along the line there will have to be give and take.

TIGER AND SNAKE

Although the basic nature of these two individuals is very different, they do share one thing in common, which is the ability to carry on happily if things are going their way. Since for most of the time this would be the same way, the Tiger and the Snake would probably get on together rather well. True, the Snake is a little more lazy by nature than the Tiger, and it would be fair to say in reverse that the Tiger lacks the laid-back success potential of the Snake. But such differences meet each other in a mutual appreciation society that is as firm as it is surprising. This is a regular match and usually a good one.

TIGER AND HORSE

This match is generally seen to be a good one and this stems from the the fact that both types have a very positive outlook on life and probably look at things in more or less the same way. There are good powers of communication here, even though the Tiger is the quieter of the two. But with this matching, the Horse understands the need for his or her Tiger mate to have short periods of solitude and makes allowances for the fact. The common abode may well be full of books, unruly children and a kind of love that comes into the world all too rarely. Certainly not a matching that everyone would understand, but no less positive for that fact.

TIGER AND GOAT

If there is success for the taking here, it comes about in a rather extraordinary way. The Goat tends to be a fairly quiet type and the Tiger is generally supposed to be more gregarious. Basically this is true, and yet there is something in the Tiger type that understands a simpler and more quiet way to live and love. As a result this pairing often works out rather well. The two people concerned are likely to be good friends and although there is much that they do not share in common, both can make a positive appraisal of the fact and learn a great deal as a result. Sexual sense may not be the important spur here.

TIGER AND MONKEY

Perhaps not the most likely match at first sight, after all, these signs are just about as different as it is possible for two individuals to be. All the same, it would not be sensible to rule the possibility out, even though there are certain to be difficulties on the way to happiness. The Monkey likes to lord it over everyone, which does not please the Tiger at all. Yet Monkey types are very attractive and the Tiger may find a certain fascination that is difficult to explain, and yet very compulsive. Monkeys are also more materialistic than Tiger types, but on an intellectual level the Tiger can probably ignore this fact and live an abstemious life all the same.

TIGER AND ROOSTER

This pairing could turn out to be as funny as it is unlikely. Tigers are inclined to do their own thing, of this there is no doubt. This leaves the poor Rooster flapping about in a terrible state, because to this type there is nothing half so important in life as a state of order. Whilst the Tiger tends to be a thinker, the Rooster wants to get things done. There might be a level at which these differing qualities could be brought together and achieve a degree of overall success, but there is almost certain to be a wealth of fur and feathers flying before the destination is reached. If this union really does become secure almost anything is possible!

TIGER AND DOG

It has been shown time and again in this book just how adaptable the Dog person is, and for this reason, if for no other, the Dog takes up the slack in almost any potential relationship. In this case however the Tiger is likely to contribute too because he or she should instinctively realise just what a treasure the Dog person actually is. True, the pair may get little done outside of talking about it, but even if this results in a disorganised life, this is not to infer any lack of happiness. In this home, look for a stack of unpaid bills - not through lack of cash, but as a result of bad organisation.

TIGER AND PIG

Tiger people worry Pig types, and there is no getting away from the fact. Although the Pig is not as tied to routine as the Rooster we still find a person here who wants to plan ahead and who appreciates some prior warning of any event. The Tiger individual does not understand this need at all and is likely to descend at any hour of the day or night with a dozen friends in tow. The sensual quality of the Pig could interest a Tiger, especially at a sexual level, but in other respects the Tiger is no great lover of the 'physical' in life. We have a possible match here, but probably not of the best kind. A little give and take might help the situation.

RABBIT AND RABBIT

An ideal relationship this one. What a pity then that we do not live in a world of ideals. The problem is that the Rabbit is so very sensitive by nature, and two Rabbit types together will at least double this tendency. Virtually nothing would be said if there were any possibility of offering offence, and no radical views would be hurled across the dining table in this house. Love would be present in great quantity, but what are this pair going to spread on the bread? A world of ideals is fine, as long as someone gets round to doing something now and again. The real difficulty here is that two Rabbits create a beautiful room, but with no real floor to stand on!

RABBIT AND DRAGON

You could be forgiven for believing that the fiery Dragon would eat up the poor Rabbit in a moment and yet, unlikely as it might seem, this relationship stands a very good chance of working. Outright materialism can meet total spirituality, as long as there is goodwill on both sides. Each side of this pairing prepares its opposite for worlds that are not natural, but which could appear attractive. Give this couple a few years and you might find that they have swapped so much of each other, that they now appear to be one functioning whole. This relationship might just be fated to succeed wonderfully.

RABBIT AND SNAKE

Some relationships turn out to be very demanding, but can be successful all the same. This coming together is certainly not of that variety, but rather stands a good chance of working out for the opposite reason. Neither the Rabbit or the Snake ask much more out of life than a little happiness and something to eat now and again. It might turn out that both would demand so little of each other that there would be no cohesion to bond the pairing and yet there are many examples of this combination working out just fine. Still the chance of one or other party wandering cannot be ruled out and some sort of effort really should be made by both parties.

RABBIT AND HORSE

If anyone is going to force the sensitive Rabbit out of its burrow and into the real world of concrete happenings it is likely to be the Horse type. The greatest potential here is in the liberation that is offered to the Rabbit part of the combination, whilst the Horse person gains through having a partner who is likely to prove very understanding and quite able to deal with the strange behaviour that Horse people are capable of displaying. The Horse individual manages to offer more confidence to the Rabbit type, which although a sure-fire path to initial success could just mean that the Rabbit, having found its feet, uses them to totter off somewhere else!

RABBIT AND GOAT

There should be little difficulty here, if only because both these signs are natural homemakers and would do their very best to keep each other happy all the time. Life would be very comfortable inside the cocoon of this relationship and family matters would be of supreme importance. The love generated may well be of a more domestic type and probably would not be the archetype for monumental passion. Nevertheless the Rabbit and the Goat would have their moments, for both are quite sexually motivated at heart. Boredom would have to be dealt with at some stage however.

RABBIT AND MONKEY

Monkey types are very kind at heart and so the sensitive Rabbit would feel comforted and protected by the hug that would be on offer. Conversely, the Rabbit could certainly bring a degree of intuition and more understanding of the deeper qualities of a Monkey partner than most other sign types would find to be possible. In the end though it might be hard for the Monkey not to try and dominate the relationship, even if this is not at all intentional. As long as this turns out to be fine by the Rabbit, then things should still work out well. A liberated Rabbit would present a different picture altogether though and would be harder for the Monkey to deal with.

RABBIT AND ROOSTER

Rabbit people would do almost anything for a peaceful life, and although both the Rabbit and the Rooster are thinkers, there is nothing peaceful about a Rooster person who is in full swing and who seems determined to turn the whole world upside down. Peace and quiet is not the greatest gift on offer in any chicken run, which might, in the fullness of time, drive the poor Rabbit completely round the bend. Both signs tend to be fairly good earners and this is particularly true in the case of the Rooster. It might be suggested that this relationship is more likely to work if the Rabbit is the male half of the combination.

RABBIT AND DOG

Generally speaking, and if both parties are true to their sign, there is every potential here for immediate and lasting success. This stems from the fact that these types are naturally so happy in each other's company. There would be plenty of chatter going on all the time and the open-minded Dog type would be more than able to cope with some of the more 'far out' ideas put forward by the average Rabbit. Each of these signs takes very well to married life and both make good parents. The mutual home would reflect both parties and at a sexual level there would be a good understanding established early on. An easygoing pair this and probably ideally suited.

RABBIT AND PIG

Another potentially good combination. Instinctively the Rabbit and the Pig understand each other and this surely must be the best basis for lasting happiness within any sort of relationship. Intuition would play an important part in the bonding, from both directions, and there is little doubt that great love could be generated by both parties. Where ideas and ideals do not match, both the Rabbit and the Pig are flexible enough to allow for the fact and in any case much cross-fertilisation turns out to be the order of the day here. This may be as true behind closed doors as it is at a practical level because the physical side of this relationship is of great importance. The Rabbit and the Pig are capable of great happiness.

DRAGON AND DRAGON

Stand back and watch the sparks fly if you consider this to be a workable commodity. Remember first that the Dragon is by far and away the most dominant of all Chinese signs. Multiply this fact by two and then realise that explosions are certain to occur. Not that this rules out the possibility, because the two characters would certainly have many points of reference and would probably form a mutual appreciation society that could do much to defuse the potential bomb. There are gains financially, since Dragons are usually good earners, whilst the sex life of this pair would be passionate, exciting and very physical. As parents two Dragons together would almost certainly co-operate.

DRAGON AND SNAKE

The Dragon and the Snake should be able to forge a reasonably happy life together, though it is likely that the Snake would be expected to take a back seat in the decision making right from the start. Of course this really doesn't matter because the wily Snake has his or her own way of ruling the roost, and the less intellectual Dragon might not even realise that this was happening. As the Dragon type flew around, breathing fire in all directions, the far more detached Snake would watch from a distance and wait until the fuel was exhausted.

DRAGON AND HORSE

We have here the makings of an interesting, vibrant and really quite cheerful match. The Horse type is a communicator, and since the Dragon is not averse to having his or her own say too, then at least there would be plenty to talk about in this coming together. The Horse is charming and is able to defuse potential difficulties before they actually cause trouble, which is always a good potential when dealing with the rather irrational Dragon. Action comes from the scaly half of this relationship, funded by the continual good ideas that the Horse type can supply. Look for a sex life that would be imaginative and interesting and a family life that could turn out to be anything but conventional.

DRAGON AND GOAT

If the Goat in this potential match is of the type who responds to being looked after, all should go well. The potential problem would come along on those occasions when the Goat person decided that it was time for him or her to have their say. Chances are that by the time this happens, the Dragon has become so used to ruling the relationship that difficulties might begin to emerge. It would certainly be sensible for the Goat to exert a little authority right from the word go. A very positive factor would be the ability of the calm Goat to bring a slightly more steady set of routines into the hectic incarnation that is the Dragon's lot.

DRAGON AND MONKEY

There are both high and low spots on offer with this combination, because the Dragon and the Monkey share many characteristics. Both are inclined to be very 'reactive' and each is likely to live for the moment. In many cases this would be a recipe for singular success, though it has to be said that any arguments that do arise are going to be of a very aggressive nature and probably fairly protracted. In any given situation someone has to back down, unless a compromise is found. This can be difficult with the Dragon and the Monkey. A good combination for travelling and for ringing the changes in life.

DRAGON AND ROOSTER

If there is any Chinese sign who has the capacity to clip the wings of the Dragon type it is certainly the Rooster. Life for the Dragon is a constant flurry of activity and no Dragon person ever gets the degree of rest and relaxation that he or she strictly needs. The more rational and much more steady Rooster can supply a calm environment, even if it turns out to be rather more tidy than the Dragon might choose. Much of the time this couple would live together comfortably, but bearing in mind the potential differences, they could also enjoy a fairly 'singular' sort of existence in a day-to-day sense. At least in this partnership the Dragon may live for longer!

DRAGON AND DOG

Here we have a pair of astrological opposites, and although the Dog is a very flexible and accommodating sort of person, even this basically kind person has his or her limits. For some reason Dragon people always feel a need to bully Dog types, which is something that the pleasant and well-mannered mutt would only accept for so long. On so many occasions there would be a long period of apparent harmony and then one day the Dog would decide that enough was enough. If you are the Dragon half of this combination do remember that no matter how easygoing Dog people are, they do have opinions of their own. This admission might be enough to ensure happiness.

DRAGON AND PIG

As long as a little understanding was present from both sides of this equation, the Dragon and the Pig could end up leading a happy life together. The planetary indications are very similar, even if they show themselves in radically different ways, so that there is a basic understanding and probably a willingness to accommodate difficulties that might otherwise arise. Male Dragon, female Pig is the better combination of the two, but even the reverse could work well if both parties are willing to put in a degree of effort. Sexually speaking this should be a good union, and is also fortunate for all family matters.

SNAKE AND SNAKE

If you were to live next door to this couple you might end up suspecting that you had no neighbours at all, so quiet and inoffensive this combination appears to be from the outside. Of course things are rarely what they seem, so that slowly and steadily a degree of success is being achieved between the two Snakes that the world might not suspect at all. Material gains are always likely, though like everything else they come slowly and steadily and at least there would be few arguments to rattle the scales of either party here. After a number of years this pair might even begin to look alike, and they will certainly think in the same way.

SNAKE AND HORSE

Things are not going to be easy for the Snake and the Horse and it has to be said that this is probably not the best combination for marital success. The Snake needs a degree of stability that is very difficult for the Horse type to supply, whilst the Horse is on a constant search for the sort of excitement in life that the poor Snake finds difficult to cope with. However, there are occasions when this pair would come together in a positive way by living separate lives together. This might not sound like a potential for marital bliss, but there are examples when it is so, and this could be one of them. Both signs are kind, and could at least be good friends.

SNAKE AND GOAT

Although the potential here is probably not tremendous, there are plenty of Snake and Goat types living together in great happiness and a good degree of harmony. Perhaps a slight drawback could be the fact that there is no tremendous inspiration coming from either direction so that, without a high degree of effort on both parts, the relationship could become boring. Stimulus from outside is essential and it would be no use for the Snake and Goat to crawl into their castle and pull up the drawbridge. Both signs are capable of deep and lasting love and would manage to create a happy family home.

SNAKE AND MONKEY

An unusual combination this one, but probably a union that might indicate success at many levels. True the Monkey likes to get his or her own way, and it is also fair to say that the Snake can be fairly stubborn if this situation goes against the grain. But for all this the Monkey is not a bully and has a basically kind disposition, which suits the Snake down to the ground. The Snake would probably be the natural home-builder here and would want to make things as comfortable as possible, whilst the Monkey is not quite so interested in domestic details. A good intellectual meeting and possibly a deep and lasting friendship.

SNAKE AND ROOSTER

Both these signs really do understand the necessary components of life and deal with eventualities in almost entirely the same way. For this reason, if for no other, this ought to be a happy union. The home of this pair would be comfortable, and perhaps even a little too comfortable for some other sign types. The potential for earning is good, since both the Snake and the Rooster can keep their noses to the grindstone and are good providers. Underlying the quiet exterior of both these types is a degree of sensuality that might make this combination reD-hot when behind closed doors. Even if this is so, it is unlikely that anyone else would guess.

SNAKE AND DOG

It is hard to see how this pair could ever be at odds with each other. The Dog, as we have seen, is a very adaptable type, but even this patient pooch does not have to change very much to take on board the fairly easygoing Snake. There should be great harmony here and a basic agreement over the fabric of life that could lead to a degree of happiness that some combinations of signs would never experience. A word of warning though. Excitement is necessary too, especially to the Dog, and there is the slightest potential for boredom to develop with this match.

SNAKE AND PIG

If there is a potential problem with this pairing, it does not stem from any real difference in attitude, but more from a lack of basic communication. Although both these signs are friendly enough, neither is going to drive a bulldozer through life and the likelihood for excitement is not startling. Perhaps the Snake and the Pig could make it work, but there needs to be a genuine interest in the outside world and in issues beyond the scope of the relationship. If the initial encounter is even to come about, one of these signs is going to have to take some sort of initiative. Certainly not a union that would throw up many rows, however.

HORSE AND HORSE

There is certainly going to be a great deal of action with this pair about and no lack of enthusiasm either. The Horse is a naturally gregarious type and two in the same household could just make for a successful union. The basic reason for this fact is that there is only the Horse type who would have sufficient energy to keep up with another member of the same astrological family. Both partners would have to learn a little self-control, or things could get out of hand. All the same, most aspects of life would be fun and outsiders would be welcome to join in the party atmosphere that is sure to predominate. A feast of fun for all!

HORSE AND GOAT

All that can be said about this union is 'poor Goat', although this might be a little unfair because, in the main, there is plenty of potential for a happy union here. Horse types are often attracted to the quieter and more thoughtful Goat, whilst the Goat itself is often bowled over by the sheer love of life and general enthusiasm exhibited by the Horse. Few arguments would ensue here because although there may not be a meeting of minds, there is genuine mutual appreciation. The most important thing that can be said about this relationship is that the parties concerned are very good friends.

HORSE AND MONKEY

Somewhere, deep inside themselves, Monkey people are very practical, which the poor Horse usually is not. If anything is going to cause a rift in this relationship it is likely to be the fact that the Monkey simply cannot understand why the Horse person is so fickle and often even a little scatterbrained. Of course this is not true, it simply looks that way from the tree where the Monkey is sitting. There is plenty of potential for success born out of a mutual appreciation of adventure and given time this pair might learn how to get on tolerably well. As a forced, 'desert island' type union, the Horse and the Monkey would have all the ingredients for a joyful time.

HORSE AND ROOSTER

In an astrological sense the Horse and the Rooster do have something in common because they are ruled by the same planet. But when you have said that you have probably said it all. Horse people infuriate tidy, steady-minded Roosters, who cannot come to terms with the erratic comings and goings of the much more adventurous Horse. Why does he or she make crumbs all over the carpet, or dash about as if the world was going to end tomorrow? These are Rooster questions concerning the Horse. Meanwhile, the nag has little to say on the subject, since he or she is too busy making an even bigger mess for the Rooster to clear up. And that may be exactly what the Rooster type really wants from life!

HORSE AND DOG

When outsiders meet this couple for the first time, and observe the degree of affection and mutual understanding that exists between them, there is often a warm response to the situation. The Horse and Dog types together have the capacity, not only to make each other happy, but the rest of the world too. The shortfall of one is the strong point of the other, and this works in both directions. All the same, both signs are a little flighty and so there are bound to be ups and downs on the way.

HORSE AND PIG

If there is a problem here it probably comes more from the direction of the Pig, whose capacity for life is very different from that exhibited by the much more excitable Horse. Holidays might be a good case in question. Pig people love to lie on the beach, whilst Horse types want to be dashing round every historical and general interest location to be found. Compromise is difficult because there is a lack of basic understanding. On the reverse side of the coin the relationship could be sexually dynamic and the Pig does show a definite interest in lost causes, which a depressed Horse can sometimes seem to be. Things could easily go either way here!

GOAT AND GOAT

Since these people come from the same part of the farm in any case, there is really little reason why they should not get on tolerably well together - in a 'goaty' sort of way. This is a sensitive type, with much to offer in the way of sympathy and practical help. Perhaps two such types together might be a little 'yucky', often to be seen in public wearing matching home-knitted jumpers, or out together buying red lentils. Not that this necessarily turns out to be a bad thing, just as long as the participants are truly happy with their lot in life. A quiet household would be the result, probably heralding the arrival of a multitude of equally quiet children.

GOAT AND MONKEY

It is often the case with the Monkey, when matched against quieter and generally less dynamic signs, that a degree of force will be used in order that the Monkey can have his or her own way. Well the advice of Tung Jen in this case is 'don't try it'. The Goat is quiet - yes, and will cause nobody any bother; unless, that is, someone tries to make it do something that really goes against the grain. On the whole this is not a bad match and there are many compensations. But watch out, Mr or Miss Monkey, because your long-suffering and kind Goat is nobody's fool and will only stand so much.

GOAT AND ROOSTER

These are both fairly domestic critters it's true, and on this account the matching should be a rather good one. However, life with the Rooster could easily make the Goat type more adventurous and desirous of change, if only because the very solid Rooster is not this way at all. Certainly this would be a good relationship in bed, and that is where this couple might spend a fair amount of their time. There would be a common interest in matters domestic and a great love of family. Materially speaking conditions would be fairly comfortable, but some intellectual stimulus might be necessary in order to bring out the true potential in this pair.

GOAT AND DOG

The Goat is probably one of the quietest signs of the Chinese zodiac, and this could certainly not be said to be the case with the Dog, who probably talks on from morning until night. Herein lie the seeds of some discord. The Goat individual is often quite happy to be silent, which the Dog person simply does not understand. As a result the Goat may be accused of being 'sulky' whilst the Goat would level the charge at the Dog that he or she never stops 'chattering'. In the end one or other of the pair might just get tired of the whole business and go off to find someone else. If this one sore point can be sorted out however, there is room for success at other levels.

GOAT AND PIG

Two very sensitive types come together in this matching, which, other things considered, could make for a generally happy union. Nobody could possibly fathom the depths of this relationship from the outside and there probably isn't much room left to get inside it either. So to all of us the private world of the Goat and the Pig is a closed book, and since these are two of the most sexually motivated signs of the zodiac, it's probably a good thing. Since the windows of this home are too steamy to see through, we can only take it as read that everything inside is happy.

MONKEY AND MONKEY

This is a power struggle in the making and one that could prove very interesting when viewed from the perspective of a third party. Not that there is much room for anyone else to interfere because the Monkeys in question are never silent for long enough to allow outside influences to have a bearing on them. Look for a very reactive sort of union, with plenty of arguments but a great deal of love too. Not everyone is happy with silence and many people love the cut and thrust of discussion. The Monkey is basically kind and loving at heart, and two together doubly so - though in a rather noisy sort of way. If this is a recipe for success, it's a hot curry all the same!

MONKEY AND ROOSTER

There are some relationships that really do look unlikely, and yet experience proves that almost anything is possible with a degree of goodwill on both sides. The Monkey would almost certainly find the Rooster type to be a 'nag', whilst the Rooster could accuse the Monkey of being 'dominant and overbearing'. In reality the wily old bird is more than capable of holding its own in this attachment and a sort of grudging acceptance of the fact on the part of the Monkey type could easily follow. The pair might lead very different sorts of lives, and yet still find common accord over matters domestic. Not an especially common pairing all the same.

MONKEY AND DOG

Here we do have the basis for a happy life, if only because the two signs complEment each other at so many levels. The typical Dog person is far more assertive than might initially seem to be the case, though is probably diplomatic enough to allow the Monkey to consider that he or she rules the roost. This is all that the Monkey needs before giving back total control over almost everything in a voluntary manner. Monkeys only react if there is something to push against, which is not likely with the Dog around. In almost every way this pair could find a way to be happy and contented together, which is why so many Monkey and Dog types give it a try.

MONKEY AND PIG

If this union is one of note, the fact stems from the differences, and not the similarities of the people concerned. The Monkey and the Pig are quite unalike in many ways, and yet this fact could lead to significant happiness all the same. The Monkey is loud and fairly aggressive, whilst the Pig is quieter and mainly submissive. Monkey people are go-getters, whilst Pig types often wait for fortune to favour them. Pig individuals love luxury, but Monkey types can get by on very little. If it seems that there is no common ground here, think again. Opposites attract! It's a magnetic property that is just as likely to work with people.

ROOSTER AND ROOSTER

One thing is for certain, this is likely to be the most tidy house on the block. It's hard to say how two Roosters would manage to rub along together because, as with all matchings of identical signs, it could be very successful, or a complete disaster. What is less likely however is any situation that stands midway between the two. Roosters are caring individuals, even if they do flap about a little on the way to proving the fact, and this could be a calm relationship, interrupted by the odd common panic. Material considerations should be good, though personal clinches might be kept to a minimum. These two make marriage a business and are both executives.

ROOSTER AND DOG

The Dog person, although personally quite smart and usually fairly domesticated, is not half so caring about tidiness as the Rooster is. Part of the reason stems from the fact that the Dog would rather be out having a good time than worrying over-much about the state of the living room. At the end of the day this is what could well happen, since the Rooster is often home-bound, whilst the Dog type is not. Whether this spells a recipe for marital bliss is hard to say, but the prognosis may not be all that good. The Dog understands give and take, and can smile sweetly at the peculiarities of the Rooster.

ROOSTER AND PIG

More successful than the last example, the Rooster and the Pig understand each other fairly well. If there are any difficulties they may well stem from the overt sensuality that the Pig shows to the world, which may not turn out to be the Rooster's cup of tea. In a sexual sense the Pig is out to have a good time, whilst the Rooster might just turn out to be as tidy minded in this department of life as he or she is in any other. The Rooster could also be annoyed at the Pig's apparent desire to take life easily, which is something that the Rooster type rarely does. The sight of a marital partner with his or her feet up could have the Rooster flapping mightily.

DOG AND DOG

A success is likely here, though there are a few provisos. Dogs are kind and loving, anxious to please and very faithful - for the moment! This is not a sign that spawns people who have a great regard for themselves however and if the average Dog cannot come to terms with its own shortcomings, how is it going to feel if they are reflected back all the time? Either this union is going to afford each Dog type more confidence, or the reverse is going to be the case and self-esteem is likely to be lacking in the household. The good news is that Dogs are perceptive and adaptable. Most importantly, they can dredge up optimism, almost from nowhere.

DOG AND PIG

It is fairly rare for this combination to come together in the first place, because there may not be an initial attraction. However, if this hurdle is crossed and the pair end up living together, the prognosis is really very good. The adaptable and imaginative Dog can cope with the depth and sensuality of the Pig, whilst the porker is only too happy to view the smiling face of his or her Dog partner with tremendous affection and a growing love. If ever there was a case of 'it started quietly and grew' in Chinese compatability, we may be looking at it here. This home would be a generally happy one.

PIG AND PIG

A quiet relationship this one, with nobody to drop stones into the bottomless well that is the nature of the Pig type. Without the splash that ensues from such an action, there is no response and as a result little in the way of interesting conversation. It isn't that the Pigs concerned have nothing to say to each other, simply that the process never really gets started. Behind closed doors things might be rather different however and all the talking in the world is likely to be undertaken by two Pig bodies in the same bed. If this is enough to glue the pair together then all may turn out for the best, though even the Pig has its physical limits.

CHINESE MOON AND LOVE

The ancient Chinese believed that the duration of one Moon, that is from the New Moon on to the next New Moon, was ruled by one of the twelve animal signs. These correspond almost exactly with what advocates of Western Astrology have come to know as their 'Sun Sign'. Arguably, of all single factors in the astrological make-up of an individual, this is probably the most important. However, it should be remembered that in all forms of Astrology, it is the overall part played by all aspects that determines the nature. Work out from the table below what any Chinese Moon sign is and then read the relevant entry in the section that follows. You can also refer to the more complete descriptions of the Chinese signs at the front of the book. Together with the Animal Year sign, Element and Ascendant Sign, the Chinese Moon offers yet another insight into the way different signs live and love.

CHINESE MOONS AND WESTERN SUN SIGN COUNTERPARTS

CHINESE MOON	WESTERN SUN SIGN	OPERATIVE DATES
DRAGON	ARIES	Mar 21st - Apr 20th
SNAKE	TAURUS	Apr 21st - May 21st
HORSE	GEMINI	May 22nd - Jun 21st
GOAT	CANCER	Jun 22nd - Jul 22nd
MONKEY	LEO	Jul 23rd - Aug 23rd
ROOSTER	VIRGO	Aug 24th - Sep 23rd
DOG	LIBRA	Sep 24th - Oct 23rd
PIG	SCORPIO	Oct 24th - Nov 22nd
RAT	SAGITTARIUS	Nov 23rd - Dec 21st
OX	CAPRICORN	Dec 22nd - Jan 20th
TIGER	AQUARIUS	Jan 21st - Feb 19th
RABBIT	PISCES	Feb 20th - Mar 20th

THE RAT MOON AND LOVE

Here we find a person with a tremendous amount of energy, even if much of it is given to the more routine aspects of life, with little enough to spare for the trivialities that are necessary in cementing a relationship together. The Rat is capable of great success, though is just as likely to go bust. Not that even this is likely to deter the ever-optimistic Rat, who will simply start again from scratch, apparently with as much confidence as ever.

Understanding what makes the Rat tick is not all that difficult and this person is not hard to love, just as long as the attributes it displays are to your personal liking. The Rat can turn its light of love on almost any other sign and can, on occasions, appear to be deeply romantic. All the same it's a hit and miss sort of situation as so much depends on what is going on in other areas of life because there are only so many hours in a day - even a Rat day. Keeping up with the Jones' is fairly important to the Rat, though only as a yardstick by which to judge the level of success that has already been achieved.

THE OX MOON AND LOVE

The steady plodder of the Chinese zodiac, the careful Ox always gets where it wants to go, even if it takes a while to complete the journey. To really appreciate what the Ox has to offer a prospective partner must have a degree of patience too, which is why only certain types really take to this match. The Ox is an excellent provider, will always be on hand to help and to offer advice, and turns out to know everything about everything. If this last appears to be rather cynical, then it is not intended to be so because the Ox watches, listens and learns. Such people are generally quite artistic and are capable of creating a beautiful home, which they relish.

For many people, there could not be a better lover in the world than the Ox, who is a natural bringer of flowers and who will rarely fail to remember birthdays or Valentine's Day. If it's excitement that fires you however, this is not the person for you because although the Ox is intelligent, he or she does not have the best imagination going and does not want to ring the changes all that often.

THE TIGER MOON AND LOVE

If it is the unusual in life that fascinates you, look no further than the Tiger Moon type. This sign is hard to fathom and is typical of the sort of person who does not know him or her self all that well either. Certainly intellectual, always fascinating and rarely stuck for something to say, the Tiger does have a quiet side, and this can puzzle those who think they have come to terms with the sign. 'Does he or doesn't he? Is she or isn't she?' These sorts of questions crop up all the time when dealing with the Tiger, who can, on occasions, prove to be the most infuriating person imaginable.

What we have here is a true original, so that even within the sign there are no two Tiger people who are exactly alike, and finding the 'type' is almost impossible. The Tiger loves to read, can be very romantic, is a good and tender lover and is never violent in a physical sense. Tigers can sulk wonderfully though and need to be treated like naughty children on some occasions. In a way, this is exactly what they probably are spiritually.

THE RABBIT MOON AND LOVE

Probably one of the kindest people you would want to meet in a month of Sundays, the Rabbit Moon person is usually very affectionate, quite understanding and almost universally loveable. Do we have a paragon of virtue here then? Is there truly perfection to be found in nature? Unfortunately not! The Rabbit tends to become very confused by the simplest of personal issues, not least of all those thrown up by commitment and constancy. For some unfathomable reason the Rabbit individual often chooses entirely the wrong sort of partner in the first place and often seems to be unlucky in love. This might be an oversimplification of the situation though because the dilemmas spring from free choices, which are not always thought through fully.

Every rule has its exceptions, and in this respect the Rabbit rule is no different from any other. So much depends on other astrological characteristics in this case, that the Rabbit Moon taken alone is a poor guide to the basic nature. Certainly a person who is worth a second, long look.

THE DRAGON MOON AND LOVE

A firebrand of a person the Dragon, and certainly not cut out for just anyone to deal with. Here we have the natural leader of the world and it might be fair to suggest that half the dictators of history have been Dragon Moon people. Not that this ought to put you off unduly, it all really comes down to the sort of person that you are and what it is you are looking for in life. If you want a compliant partner, who will do your bidding without question, then the Dragon is definitely not your cup of tea. On the other hand, if you want a protective arm around your shoulder, good advice on almost any aspect of life and a hard crust that covers a genuinely soft centre, this is the person you most need.

The Dragon is invariably successful in life and is a capable and hard worker. Supplying the bacon is not usually a problem here, though a Dragon thwarted or prevented from giving his or her full potential can be an aggressive and prickly type. The Dragon wants to love deeply, and is more than capable of doing so - but only if matched with the right sort of person.

THE SNAKE MOON AND LOVE

We don't usually have the inclination to keep a snake around the house, as we would a cat or dog, to stroke and talk to. When it comes to astrological types however, the Snake Moon individual is as loveable as any domestic pet, and to some people just as necessary to their well-being. The Snake Moon person is kind and understanding, extremely laid back and very demonstrative - in a low-key sort of way. At the same time the Snake person is capable of being very practical and could probably take the whole house to pieces and put it back together again if it so chose. Although the Snake Moon type is a good talker, he or she will not be the loudest person you have ever met and is just as willing to listen to what you have to say, and to be supportive of your ideas and opinions.

Trying to push a Snake is the same as pushing a piece of rope, you are simply wasting your time. But the analogy holds true the other way round, since you can 'lead' a length of rope anywhere. Herein lies the secret of success when it comes to getting the Snake round to your point of view.

THE HORSE MOON AND LOVE

There is no doubt that the Horse Moon person loves to have fun, and as long as you are the type of person who can deal with a human dynamo and actively enjoy the cut and thrust of a changing world, then this is a person you should get on well with. There are potential problems though, not the least of which is the Horse tendency to find loyalty to be a word that it does not understand. It isn't that the Horse is ever deliberately unfaithful, things just seem to work out that way. However, if the Horse Moon individual is busy enough, happy enough and is truly fulfilled, then such a problem will probably never arise in the first place.

Those choosing to live with the Horse person need to be open-minded, and to understand that the values that are important to this type are not the same as those held in the bosom of other Chinese signs. Horse Moon folk are intellectual, physically and mentally active and love to travel as much as possible.

THE GOAT MOON AND LOVE

Although the Goat Moon person may not be the most dynamic sort of individual you will ever meet, he or she should not be underestimated either because this is a person with great integrity and a warm heart. Although generally preferring to take life rather steadily, there is an adventurous and even a dramatic quality to the sign of the Goat and such individuals are often very fond of water sports of one sort or another. Absolute enthusiasm may not seem to be evident at first sight, but the Goat is a deep type and takes time for you to get to know in quite the way you should before any real judgement is made.

The Goat Moon person is a homemaker of the first order and is almost certain to be in favour of home and family above any consideration. Being very protective of offspring, male and female types alike are good parents and usually very faithful partners. A word of caution though. Goat Moon people are not always willing to face up to the truth and may spend months or years living in a fool's paradise. Goats need to be offered a few home truths now and again.

THE MONKEY MOON AND LOVE

Anyone opting for marital bliss with the Monkey should be well aware of what they are about to take on before any sort of permanent commitment is made. True, the Monkey Moon person is quite glorious at his or her best and may well represent the most loyal and honourable type you could ever want to meet. In a very dynamic way there's almost a 'saintly' quality to the Monkey, but it is of the more excitable variety and pretty difficult to keep up with - or even to understand. The Monkey is generous, warm-hearted, and willing to see the other person's point of view - when it suits him or her to do so.

If all of this marks the Monkey person out as being rather special, then this is no more than the truth, though 'special' is sometimes difficult to live with and since the Monkey expects no less of anyone else than it is willing to supply itself, life with this character can be a little tiring. You should not lack material wealth and can be fairly certain that the Monkey will stick around, even if you are only one of this complicated person's interests in life.

THE ROOSTER MOON AND LOVE

If there is one word that describes the Rooster Moon individual better than any other, that word is 'tidy'. Here we have a person who believes the adage 'A place for everything and everything in its place'. The problem is that you might be one of the 'things', which is not a state of affairs that just anyone could take to all that readily. Be prepared to dust, clean, build and generally keep house alongside the Rooster and all should be well. If, on the other hand, you want to spend your spare time doing other things, you could be in for rather a shock. The Rooster is chatty, sociable and very domestic, but can also be awkward, cranky and downright rude on occasions.

Rooster Moon types are very practical and could sort out the entire problems of the world before lunch if necessary, and still have a ham sandwich and a glass of milk ready for you by midday. But the necessary routines of life have to be endured and not usually 'enjoyed' in the way that the Rooster singularly manages to do. This person might be a treasure, or too tedious by half.

THE DOG MOON AND LOVE

It's hard to find fault with the Dog Moon individual, and yet, when looked at fairly, there are quite a few faults to be found. Although the Dog type is warm, considerate, friendly and flexible, he or she is also inclined to jump about from pillar to post, finds it almost impossible to take any sort of decision and would endure virtually anything for the sake of a peaceful life. But the gains outweigh the losses in this case to such an extent that there is probably not a more popular person to be found anywhere, and it is so very easy to forgive the Dog almost anything. In fact this probably does little to help the Dog, who, as a result, keeps on making the same mistakes time and again.

Dog people want to please everyone all the time, which plainly is not possible. However, they are ingenious, intelligent, love to read and often make good writers. They are witty, gentle and very affectionate. And when things get really tough, like the animal they represent, they will cower in a corner for a while. This is 'a sign for all seasons'.

THE PIG MOON AND LOVE

An easy person to live with this, just as long as you are aware of certain ground rules along the path to ultimate happiness. The Pig Moon type is, above all, a lover of the sensual in life. As a result there are specific items that your mutual home should contain. Amongst these could be listed a spacious and luxurious bathroom, a well-equipped kitchen, and a bedroom that could have come straight off a film set. It's hard to visualise what could upset the Pig if these factors have been dealt with, and the Pig will offer much in return. You will be loved with great strength and endurance, since this person would follow you to the very gates of hell if necessary. The Pig Moon type is quite capable, a good worker and a sympathetic person when you are down or ill.

It's true that Pig types do have a slightly darker side to their nature, though this is usually kept under lock and key and so need not trouble you unduly, unless, that is, you are unfaithful in thought, word or deed. When push comes to shove the Pig Moon person can become very jealous.

IN CONCLUSION

Since the dawn of human history is seems as though the Chinese have been a philosophical race. But they have also been rather insular, so that much of Oriental thought never found its way to the West until comparatively recent times. Now there is a tremendous interest in thoughts, actions and concepts that were in full bloom at a period when much of the rest of the world was still in prehistoric ferment. As a result people outside of Asia are often inclined to set the Chinese apart, as being somehow very different and still rather mysterious. Chinese Astrology, with its innate sense of humour and its emphasis on the very 'human' traits that we all possess, should help to redress the balance a little. We are all born of the same species and our aspirations, no matter how they are initially expressed, are essentially identical.

Despite this it is possible that those people familiar only with the Western branch of astrology, which is rather more remote and certainly more cerebral than it's Chinese counterpart, may learn much from a walk around the Chinese animal zoo. I have tried to present Chinese astrology in a way that will be accessible to the Western mind, though this is not particularly difficult since there is something intensely 'right' about the believable and often loveable animals that inhabit it.

There is always more to learn, but our studies concerning ourselves are made that much easier if we can look at our reflection in the rock pool of life and see a smile on the picture that comes back at us. The ancient Chinese obviously could, and all their observations are suffused with compassion and understanding.

When all is said and done, perhaps the best sections of this book to study when it comes to considering human relationships generally, are those that refer to you personally. The Chinese sages of old knew all too well, that until we truly, honestly know ourselves, the rest of humanity will be a closed book to us.

With every wish for peace and prosperity - but above all happiness and love.

Tung Jen.

Opening doors to the World of books

BOOK TOKEN

Book Tokens

Book Tokens can be bought and exchanged at most bookshops